THE LOVE FORCE

Brad Steiger
with
Frances Steiger

Prentice-Hall, Inc., Englewood Cliffs, New Jersey 07632

Library of Congress Cataloging in Publication Data

Steiger, Brad.
  The love force.

Includes index.
  1. Psychical research.   2. Love—Miscellanea.
I. Steiger, Frances.   II. Title.
BF1045.L7S74   1985   133.8   85-3550
ISBN 0-13-540816-4
ISBN 0-13-540782-6   (A Reward book : pbk.)

© 1985 by Prentice-Hall, Inc., Englewood Cliffs, New Jersey 07632.
All rights reserved. No part of this book may be reproduced in any form
or by any means without permission in writing from the publisher.
Printed in the United States of America.

1 2 3 4 5 6 7 8 9 10

ISBN 0-13-540816-4

ISBN 0-13-540782-6 {A REWARD BOOK : PBK.}

Editorial/production supervision by Lori L. Baronian
Book design by Maria Carella and Lori L. Baronian
Manufacturing buyer: Frank Grieco
Cover design by Hal Siegel

This book is available at a special discount when ordered in
bulk quantities. Contact Prentice-Hall, Inc., General
Publishing Division, Special Sales, Englewood Cliffs, N.J. 07632.

Prentice-Hall International (UK) Limited, *London*
Prentice-Hall of Australia Pty. Limited, *Sydney*
Prentice-Hall Canada Inc., *Toronto*
Prentice-Hall Hispanoamericana, S.A., *Mexico*
Prentice-Hall of India Private Limited, *New Delhi*
Prentice-Hall of Japan, Inc., *Tokyo*
Prentice-Hall of Southeast Asia Pte. Ltd., *Singapore*
Whitehall Books Limited, *Wellington, New Zealand*
Editora Prentice-Hall do Brasil Ltda., *Rio de Janeiro*

CONTENTS

1
THE LOVE FORCE, 1

2
LOVE AND SEX IN THE PSYCHIC WORLD, 20

3
DREAM POWER AND DREAM LOVERS, 41

4
HEART-TO-HEART COMMUNICATION, 62

5
OUT-OF-BODY ROMANCE, 73

6
**LOVERS WHO
TRANSCENDED THE GRAVE, 89**

7
HAUNTED HOUSEHOLDS, 114

8
**JEALOUS SPIRITS
THAT WON'T LET GO, 138**

9
SEXUAL MOLESTERS FROM SHADOWLAND
The Love Force Perverted, 148

10
**MULTIDIMENSIONAL BEINGS
OF LOVE AND LIGHT, 160**

11
WE HAVE LOVED BEFORE, 174

12
STRENGTHEN YOUR OWN LOVE FORCE, 190

INDEX, 206

THE LOVE FORCE

1

THE LOVE FORCE

Mina Brant's husband, Carlyle, is a construction worker. Once, because of lack of work in the area where he lives, he was forced to take a job on a large dam project more than 400 miles from his home.

"It was the longest six months I think I have ever spent," Mina wrote. "Carlyle could get home only on weekends. He would not arrive until after midnight on Friday, and he would have to be back on the road right after the noon meal on Sunday. For those six months, we lived only on Saturdays."

Mina remembered one dreary fall day when she was particularly lonely. Clouds hung low in the sky, and a cold rain drizzled on the piles of multicolored leaves. It was the kind of day when you need to be close to someone you love. Trying hard to fight her depression, Mina pulled on a heavy sweater and sat in her cold house, pasting premium stamps in coupon books.

Mina recalled:

That night my bed felt as damp and lonely as a grave. My only consolation was that it was Thursday and Carlyle would be

> *home that next night. I lay shivering between the sheets, cursing the job situation that had taken my husband so far away from me.*
>
> *Then I thought that I felt a slight pressure on Carlyle's side of the bed. I turned over, saw nothing, but it seemed to me that I could feel a kind of warmth coming from my husband's pillow. I ran my hand along the inside of the bedclothes, and I concluded that I must be losing my grip on reality—Carlyle's side of the bed definitely felt warm, like he had been sleeping there and had just got up.*
>
> *I lay on my side of the bed for a few moments longer, then, once again, I slid my hand over the sheet.*
>
> *There could be no mistaking it. The bed on Carlyle's side was as warm as toast. It had been a cold, lonely day, and I had no interest in trying to figure out why that side of the bed should be so warm when no one was sleeping there. Without another moment's hesitation, I slid over into the blessed pocket of warmth and comfort and fell asleep almost at once.*

Mina did not think of the strange incident again until three days later when she and her husband were eating their farewell Sunday meal.

Carlyle's response to her story about the strangely warm bed was hardly what she had expected. He stared at her for a few moments in complete silence, then spoke to her in slow measured sentences.

It seems that Carlyle Brant had been lying in the construction worker's bunkhouse on that same Thursday night, trying to come to terms with his own loneliness. If he had had his own car, he told his wife, he would have chucked it all, job or no job, and come home to her right then.

That night as he lay there surrounded by his snoring companions, his entire being seemed suffused with personal anguish. He wanted so much to be in his own clean bed, to be able to feel his wife sleeping beside him. He told Mina:

> *I decided to experiment. I wanted to see if it were possible to will myself home over those 400 miles. I rested my hands behind*

my head and summoned every drop of concentration that I had inside my brain. I thought of nothing but you and home.

There was a kind of rushing sensation, and I stood beside our bed looking down at you. You were lying there, looking kind of sad, not yet sleeping.

I slipped in beside you, and you moved your hand over me. A few minutes later, you did it again. I thought that you knew I lay there, because you rolled over and snuggled up next to me. I put my arm around you, and we both went right to sleep.

Carlyle awakened back in the bunkhouse that next morning, just as Mina awakened alone in her bed back home. "But we will always wonder if Carlyle really did come home that night," Mrs. Brant wrote, "or if our deep love enabled us to share a dream so that we could experience a moment of comfort when we were both longing so terribly for each other."

A growing number of scientific researchers are becoming convinced that experiences like the one described by Carlyle and Mina Brant may truly be more than dreams.

Out-of-body experiences, dramatic examples of telepathic transfer, astonishing dreams, and remarkable accounts of spirit visitations may, according to dramatic case histories gathered during my more than twenty-five years as a psychical researcher, be energized by the greatest power in the universe—love. Of all the seen and unseen forces that move men and women, none is more powerful than the Love Force, and I have come to believe that the primal impulse of sexual desire has produced some of the most astounding examples of physical phenomena in the entire literature of the paranormal.

Since the mid-1960s, during interviews with those men and women gifted with psi abilities telepathy, clairvoyance, precognition, mediumship), I have been asking questions concerning sex, love, and psychic phenomena. Many interviewees have responded to my queries in a frank and open manner, and I have found general agreement to the hypothesis that was concisely stated by Oscar W. Firkins in his *Memoirs and Letters:* "Mysticism and sex have been frequent associates because they are kindred."

In addition to stories from my dozens of interviewees, I have received hundreds of stories recounting a blend of the Love Force and psi phenomena from readers of my books, from personal consultations, and from participants in the awareness seminars that my wife, Frances Paschal Steiger, and I conduct throughout the United States and in many foreign countries.

In this book I am going to share many of these stories with you. I hope that you find them interesting in themselves, but my purpose in telling them goes beyond a mere wish to retail anecdotes. In fact, the stories fall into several definite, recognizable patterns, and it is by understanding these patterns that we can gain our greatest insights into how the Love Force both enhances psi and operates through it.

To help make the patterns clearer, I have grouped all the stories into categories. The broadest categories are represented by chapters, smaller categories by clusters of narratives within each chapter. After each story, or cluster of related stories, I give you both my comments on the events just recounted and my analysis of their significance.

As we go along, and you become increasingly familiar with the major patterns, you will find that my comments move increasingly *away* from analysis and *toward* application. That is deliberate. My real purpose is *not*—as in a textbook—to treat the psychic dimension of the Love Force as some sort of academic abstraction, but to acquaint you with its practical side, to show you how it can actually be controlled, enhanced, and made to work for *you*.

Toward the end of the book are many specific exercises and step-by-step instructions that will help you better to command (and be commanded by) the awesome power of the Love Force. But that's for later on. Right now, let's begin with a story.

Opal Blanchard used to tease her husband that their love would have to last forever because her wedding ring was so tight that she would never be able to get it off her finger.

"And that's the way it'll stay until I tell you differently," Jerry would always reply with a chuckle.

There were few things to laugh and to tease about in 1944, especially if one were the wife of a serviceman. In November of that year, Jerry Blanchard was shipped to the European theater of action, and his wife decided to live with his parents on their old farm homestead in New England.

The Blanchards treated their daughter-in-law with warmth and consideration, and they gave her Jerry's old room, complete with his own stone fireplace. Each night at dusk Mrs. Blanchard built a roaring fire on the grate, and in the morning she revived the cherry-red coals with fresh fuel.

The progress of the war in Europe dominated nearly every dinnertime conversation, and by mid-January 1945 things were going badly for the Allies. The Nazis seemed to sense that they had lost the war, and they were determined to make the Allies pay dearly for their victory.

A letter from Jerry arrived, and Opal read it aloud to his parents. Although censorship requirements would not allow him to be specific, Jerry wrote in general terms about preparations for a major offensive.

Two nights after she had received the letter from her husband, Opal remembers going to sleep filled with prayerful concern for Jerry's safety.

"I prayed for an awfully long time," she recalls, "then I fell asleep watching the flames swirl up the stone chimney."

She awakened sometime that night, her entire being suffused with terrible cold.

> *I felt cold and clammy clear to the bone. I sat up in bed to see if the fire had gone out, and I saw Jerry standing there. His features were clearly distinguishable in the red glow of the fireplace, and he looked tired and sad. He just stared at me for the longest time, then he leaned over and gently slipped my wedding ring off my finger. I'll never forget how cold his hands felt. He opened his mouth as if he were going to speak to me; then he disappeared.*

Opal blinked her eyes in disbelief and looked around at the familiar fixtures of her room, seeking reassurance of reality.

The fire in the grate was very low. It would soon be morning. She pulled the heavy quilts over her shivering frame and lay in silence until she heard the morning sounds of the Blanchard family shaking off sleep. When she was certain that everyone was up and assembled in the kitchen for breakfast, she came out to tell the family of her strange dream of Jerry.

"That was no dream," Jerry's grandmother said, shaking her head wisely. "Our poor Jerry is dead."

Opal protested. It had been only a dream, nothing more.

"Then where is your wedding ring?" Grandmother wanted to know. "Where is that ring that none of us has ever seen you remove?"

Opal clutched her hands together as if she could somehow prevent the ring's escape. She looked at her ring finger for the first time since she had awakened, and she was startled to see that it no longer bore the wedding band that had so tightly encircled it.

They found her wedding ring on the dresser, and Opal could offer no explanation of how the snug band had been removed from her finger. Grandmother insisted that the explanation had already been told: The spirit of Jerry had removed it when he had come to say goodbye.

Two weeks later a telegram arrived from the War Department, informing them of Jerry Blanchard's death in military action. He had been killed on February 8. The image of Jerry had appeared to his wife shortly after that, on February 9.

The preceding case is made all the more interesting because of the apparition's physical action of removing the tight ring from the woman's finger and transporting it to the dresser.

One might argue, of course, that Opal Blanchard, had upon receiving a telepathic impression of her dying husband, externalized an apparition of him and removed the ring herself in a kind of somnambulistic trance state. But to insist that the whole matter belongs in the realm of coincidence seems to constitute an argument woefully lacking in substance, an argument satisfactory only to the most devout skeptic.

The fact that Mrs. Blanchard had such a dream of her husband removing her wedding band, thus symbolizing the termination of their earthly bond, on the very day of his death in a land thousands of miles away, definitely suggests a strong telepathic link between dying husband and anxious wife.

There is a third story that suggests yet another aspect of how the Love Force and the paranormal may be connected.

Jane Davies and Victor Mayer had been sweethearts since their puppy-love days back in elementary school in the 1960s. Jane's parents were transferred to another city when she and Victor were juniors in high school, and the two young people were heartbroken at the thought of a separation of several hundred miles.

At first they talked of running away together and getting married, but common sense prevailed. They would write each other religiously and visit each other during every holiday. They would attend the same college after graduation from high school, where they would then be able to continue their romance as more mature young people.

One night after the teenagers had been separated for about two months, Victor looked up from his homework, distracted by what he thought must be a wisp of smoke drifting toward him.

After dinner he had lain down on his bed with his social studies book in his hands. Mom's good cooking and the extra laps at the track that afternoon had begun to take their toll on his ability to concentrate. He had just been drifting off to sleep when he was snapped back to full awareness by strange tendrils of smoke moving toward him.

His first thought was that there might be a fire in the house, but he could not smell anything burning. He knew that he should get up to investigate, but he felt strangely apathetic, almost immobile. He was content to lie still and watch the mysterious smoke swirl about in the air.

Within a few moments the smoke had congealed into a cloud; then the cloud began to take on the figure of a woman. Soon features were discernible, and Victor was shocked to recognize his beloved sweetheart, Jane. He wrote later:

> *I could not believe my eyes, I rubbed at my face with my palms and ground my fists in my eyes. I had to make sure that I was not dreaming or that I had not fainted.*
>
> *I got off my bed and started toward the cloudy thing that had become Janie. Before I could touch it, however, it gave me a sad smile and disappeared. I was compeltely dumbfounded. I sat back on my bed, feeling like all the blood had been drained from my body.*

Victor had acquired the habit of keeping a daily journal in which he recorded all significant personal experiences. When he had regained his emotional control, he went to his desk and recorded the date and the hour at which he had seen the apparition.

Two days later, Victor's parents received word that Jane Davies and her older sister had been killed when the car in which they had been riding had stalled on the tracks at a railroad crossing as the driver tried to beat the engine. The time of Jane Davies' death corresponded exactly to the time that Victor had recorded the appearance of the apparition.

The alert reader will have noticed that the people who reported the three cases just presented have had one important physical condition in common: Each of them perceived the apparition of a loved one while in bed—either just awakening from or just drifting into sleep. As one investigates accounts of such apparitions—and, indeed, many other manifestations of paranormal phenomena—one is struck with the realization of what fertile psychic ground lies in the hypnagogic state, that nebulous area that lies somewhere between waking and sleeping.

Many researchers have theorized that during this psychic "twilight zone" a person's unconscious is able to free itself from the inhibiting influence of conscious thought and become more aware and more in tune with the various mental impressions that may be vying for attention.

William Mandel and Eve Shields had known each other for several years and had become good friends long before they had begun to think of each other as potential lovers. When that awareness came, it came suddenly, to both at once, and seemed so natural and overwhelming that they could not help chiding themselves for the three years of high school, four years of college, and two years working together in the same insurance company that they had wasted.

William pronounced solemnly around the stem of his pipe that a Force-Greater-Than-They had seen fit to keep them apart, yet together, for nine years. Eve sometimes blushed at the memories of the many past occasions when she had taken her love-life problems to trusty William, who, at that time, had seemed like an older brother in whom she could confide.

When William proposed marriage, Eve did not hesitate to say yes. They had not fallen in love; they had grown in love.

Two months before the wedding, in August 1973, William was killed in an automobile accident.

> *I was left to try to assemble the scattered pieces of what seemed to be a shattered life. It was nearly a year before I began dating again, but three months after I had begun to go somewhat steadily with Owen Laverty, he asked me to marry him. I was unable to give him an answer at the time, and I asked for a few days to consider his proposal. I felt that I could love Owen, but I also felt that I did not wish to marry him just then.*

Eve explained her feelings to Owen, but the man continued to court her for nearly two years. Finally Eve agreed to marry her persistent suitor.

Then, less than a week before the wedding, Eve recalled,

> *I lay tossing and turning in bed, unable to sleep. My mind was full of thoughts of William, my dead fiance, rather than Owen, my living husband-to-be. My entire being seemed to be permeated by a strange uneasiness. How I wished that William might be there to discuss the matter with me, to give me sage counsel as he had so often in the past. In spite of myself, I began to weep.*
>
> *In between my sobbings, I was certain that I could hear William's voice calling my name. I sat bolt upright in bed, struck with the sudden realization that I was not imagining the sound of his voice; I was actually hearing William calling to me!*
>
> *I looked in the direction from which the voice seemed to be coming, and I was startled to see William standing solid as life next to my dresser. So many images began to flood my brain that I nearly succumbed to the shock of seeing William standing there.*
>
> *Then I became strangely pacified at the sound of William's voice. "Your marriage to Owen is a serious mistake," he told me. "You must not marry Owen Laverty. He is not the man for you. He is not what he appears to be."*

Eve was so moved by the apparition of her dead fiance that she feigned illness and told Owen that they must postpone their marriage to give her time to recuperate.

Two weeks later Owen Laverty was arrested on a charge of illegally possessing marijuana, heroin, and cocaine. During his hearing, evidence was produced that convicted Laverty of being a drug dealer. It was also revealed that Owen was already married and had a wife in an asylum. That poor woman, whose existence had been previously unknown to Eve, had become a drug addict under the ministrations of Owen Laverty. Eve wrote:

> *Two years later, when Tom Shields asked me to marry him, I felt almost certain that an apparition of William Mandel, my dear friend and lover, would once again appear to let me know if my choice was a wise one.*
>
> *Three nights before our August 1978 wedding, William appeared in my room. He looked just as solid as he had when he materialized two years before. I was not shocked this time, and I waited eagerly for some sign of communication from him.*
>
> *This time William only smiled, waved a hand, and disappeared. I knew that dear William had given our marriage his blessing.*

There seems to be a definite relationship between the sex drive and ESP, and this is borne out even in the sterile atmosphere of the laboratory.

It has been demonstrated that, on the average, a man is more effective as an agent (sender) of a telepathic impression and a woman is more effective as a percipient (receiver). Laboratory tests have also shown that percipients of either sex usually achieve better results if the agent is of the opposite sex. Such correlations apply to spontaneous instances of telepathy and psychic phenomena as well as to roles assumed for laboratory testing.

Shortly before her marriage to Brian O'Donnell in February 1969, Ellen Sterling was warned by some of her fiancé's friends that Margaret, his deceased wife, had sworn that she would haunt him if he should ever remarry.

Ellen thought the statement in bad taste but simply smiled

and expressed her wish that Margaret would understand and leave them in peace.

On their first night in Brian's home after their honeymoon, however, Ellen began to reconsider the women's idle chatter from the standpoint of an ominous prediction that had been realized.

They were just preparing for bed when they both heard a violent thumping from the room that Margaret O'Donnell had occupied in the last months of her illness. Margaret had suffered a stroke and had been left unable to speak; whenever she wished something, she had been forced to knock on the wall to call attention to her needs.

Brian mumbled something about a loose shutter, but Ellen noticed that he was very pale and visibly shaken. At last he breathed a deep sigh, as if he firmly regretted the age-old tradition that husbands are supposed to investigate all strange night noises. He fastened the belt of his bathrobe securely about his waist, then stepped out into the hall.

Ellen sat nervously on the edge of the bed. She had resolved to give up smoking, but Brian's pack of cigarettes on the nightstand was about to be looted. Then the noise, the terrible pounding, stopped.

She turned to glance at the door and was startled to see a colorless, bony hand reach around the doorjamb and shut out the lights. She sat on the edge of the bed screaming until Brian entered the room and snapped on the lights.

There were no further manifestations that night, but Ellen told her husband the next morning at breakfast that she did not want to sleep another night in that bedroom. Brian agreed and said that as soon as he returned from work that night he would help her move the furniture to a back bedroom.

Brian had not been out the door a minute when a flurry of knockings and thumpings sounded throughout the house. The venetian blinds shook as if they were caught in a heavy breeze. Ellen was certain that she could hear the sounds of things being moved about in the attic. Ellen told me:

> *At that time, I did not think that I would be able to go on living in that house. There was something living in the shadows that did not want me there.*

> *For several days the pattern never varied. There would be the thumpings at bedtime, the knockings and scrapings during the day. On a number of occasions, as I worked in the kitchen, I heard what sounded like a sick person dragging her feet up the stairs. Whenever I would push open the kitchen door and look up the stairs, however, there would never be anyone there.*

Ellen had tolerated the eerie manifestations for more than a week when, one day, she heard a loud pounding from Margaret's bedroom. She put down her sewing and glanced up the stairway. There had been a departure from what she had come to accept as part of the haunting's regular schedule. Up until that time, the pounding from the bedroom had sounded only at bedtime.

Ellen continued to watch the top of the stairs. If she had not known that she was alone in the house, she would have sworn that there truly was an invalid in that bedroom who was trying desperately to signal her. The longer that Ellen concentrated on the sounds, the more she became convinced that the spirit of Margaret was actually attempting to communicate with her. Ellen continued:

> *I'll never know how I summoned the courage to do so but I walked up the stairs and entered the bedroom where Margaret had lived her last days. I don't know what I expected to see. I guess I thought that I might be confronted with the ghostly image of the poor sick woman whose place I had taken.*
>
> *The room still had an antiseptic smell to it, and it had received only a cursory cleaning after Margaret's death. I stood there in the middle of the room, not really having the faintest idea what my next move might be.*
>
> *A loud thud sounded next to the bed where the dying woman must have lain and rapped out her pitiful signals to the part-time maids that Brian had barely managed to afford. I turned quickly, nearly losing my balance.*
>
> *An envelope seemed to flutter down from somewhere like an autumn leaf dropping from a tree. I picked it up and saw that it was a letter that Margaret had written to Brian. It was sealed, and from all appearances had never been opened and had never been read by the man to whom it had been sent.*

> That night I showed the letter to Brian, and hesitantly he took the envelope from my hands. Tears streamed unashamedly down his cheeks as he read the letter.
>
> When he had regained his composure, he told me that Margaret must have written the letter just hours before her death. In her own words she told him how much she loved him and that she prayed that he would forgive her for some of the selfish and thoughtless things that she had said in bitterness at the onset of her illness.
>
> When she had been deprived of her voice after the stroke, Margaret had written, she had been forced to do more listening and more thinking. She had hoped that he would remarry if she died, but she begged him to always remember her with kindness and to think only of the good days that they had shared.

According to Ellen O'Donnell, she and Brian still live in the same house, but she has never again heard the eerie knockings and the strange thumpings from Margaret's old room.

"I don't really think the surviving personality of my husband's first wife was trying to drive me away," she said, "but I do think that she wanted to make her position clear to me and to Brian. It was as though she would not permit, or sanction, our marriage until Brian had read her last letter to him."

There are cases reported in which the astral double of a loved one has brought a forewarning of danger or has interacted with an individual in such a manner as to save his life.

Martha Pilgrim remembers her father as a great sportsman, a man who loved to be the first hunter into a field whenever a new season opened. Martha's mother had no objections to her husband's pleasure in hunting, but she did object quite strongly to the fact that he and his friends stopped by a particular bar and grill for an early breakfast so that they might lace their morning coffee with some Irish whiskey. Martha writes:

> I was thirteen that season of 1956 and I can remember Pop noisily assembling all his gear to join his friends at Tony's grill.

Mom just stayed in bed, because she knew Pop wouldn't be eating breakfast before he left. Since Pop had made so much racket, I decided that I might as well get up and get my homework out of the way for the weekend. I thought that if I got all my work done, Mom might reverse her decision to not allow me to go to the matinee that day.

I had finished breakfast and was working at the kitchen table when Pop stormed into the house, livid. I had never seen him so angry.

"Where's your mother?" he yelled at me. "Never has she done so foul a thing to me!"

I told Pop that Mom was still in bed, and he moved over to me as if he might strike me. "So now she has you doing her lying for her too, eh? Did I get back to the house before her?"

I insisted that Mom lie in her bed and told Pop to go look. The keys for our second car hung on their hook beside the kitchen door. Neither of us had left the house for even a minute.

What with Pop banging his fist on the table and stomping around in the kitchen, it was not long before Mom came out of the bedroom to see what was the matter. She stood in the doorway of the kitchen, fastening her bathrobe and stifling a yawn.

All the color just kind of drained out of Pop's face. It was obvious even to a man as angry as he that Mom was just getting up. He poured himself a cup of coffee and drank it with shaking hands. Then he told us what had happened to him that morning.

"I was sitting in Tony's with the fellows when I saw Mom sitting across the room. She was the only woman in the bar, and it was crowded with hunters. I felt embarrassed, and the fellows at our booth started teasing me about the old lady checking up on me. Every time I'd try to catch Mom's eye, she smiled and turned away from me, like she was pretending not to see me.

"Finally I got up from the table and went over to her and asked her just what she was trying to do to me. But she *wouldn't answer. She just smiled and got up and walked out of the bar.*

"The fellows started ribbing me about how henpecked I was, how I couldn't even stop by for some Irish coffee without my wife checking up on me. I got so mad I told them I was going to follow Mom home and find out just what her big idea had been. But now, I find that you've never been out of bed." Pop *slumped forward in his chair, took his head between his hands, and said, "Am I losing my mind?"*

Mom told him that it must have been some other woman, but Pop answered that he should know his own wife after living with her for sixteen years. Pop was convinced that he had been given some strange omen, and he decided not to rejoin his friends. He called Tony's grill and found out that they had already left without him and had told the bartender where Pop could locate them.

Martha remembers that her father accompanied her to the matinee that day, one of the few times that the two of them had ever attended a motion picture together. They stopped after the picture and had some ice cream, and Martha felt a closeness to her father that she had not experienced for some time. Her father even joked about that morning. He confessed to his daughter that he probably would have drunk too much if he had gone with the men.

When they returned home that afternoon, Martha and her father found her mother sitting on the sofa weeping. She had just heard on the local news that all of Pop's hunting companions had been killed in a head-on collision as they had been returning home.

"Pop always felt that he had been spared for some reason," Martha Pilgrim states. "He believed that it must have been his guardian angel that had assumed Mom's shape on that morning in order to keep him home and out of that death car. He never went hunting again."

In the February 1968 issue of *Psychology Today*, Rollo May states in his provocative article, "The Daemonic: Love and Death," that he defines the daemonic as" . . . any natural function in the individual which has the power of taking over the whole person."

15

In May's definition:

> ... *Eros is the daemon which constitutes man's creative spirit, the drive that not only impels him to sexual union and to other forms of love, but also incites in him the yearning for knowledge and drives him to seek union with the truth, to become poet or artist, or scientist. Sex and eros, anger and rage, and the craving for power are daemonic and thus* either *creative or destructive. When this power goes awry, and one element takes over the total personality, we see "daemon possession," the traditional term through history for psychosis. Then we see the destructive activities of the daemonic which are the reverse side of its constructive vitality.*

I believe that eros (sex) denied, frustrated, and repressed has precipitated the psychic dissociation responsible for many alleged supernatural occurrences. This dissociated mental fragment, motivated by primitive ideas and desires, generally derives its energy source from the erotic recesses of the soul and, being the result of frustrated sexual and creative activity, represents the destructive, the violent, and the perverse side of man's transcedent level of mind and of the Love Force. This dissociated mental fragment, this projected bundle of repressions, is a product of man's psyche and is thereby capable of ignoring the conventional barriers of time and space. It may behave as a child or an ignorant person and toss objects about the room and smash pieces of furniture. It may form other voices and other personalities. It may personify itself as a "demon lover."

At eleven o'clock one night in November 1968, a Wisconsin coed was lying in her bed, drifting off to sleep. With some irritation, she became aware that something was pulling at her bedclothes, then tugging at her leg. She opened her eyes to see a hideous, hairy creature, grinning lustfully at her and pulling her slowly across the bed. She told one of my correspondents:

> *I was paralyzed. I could neither move nor cry out. There was no mistaking what plans the grotesque male creature had in mind for me. Then I thought very intensely, "God save me!" There was a very brilliant flash of light at the ceiling, and the creature disappeared. I wore a cross for a long time after that.*

Another young woman from Colorado reports that she was falling asleep with a book in her hand one night when she felt someone or something enter her room. She said:

> *Whatever it was it picked me up and tossed me in the air. I landed on the opposite side of the bed from the one I had been lying on. The door to the bathroom slammed shut, and I lay on the bed physically and emotionally drained. I lay there a long time before I had enough strength to get up. I was very frightened.*

A young career woman from San Diego, California, writes that one night immediately after she had turned off her bedlamp, she heard a buzzing sound around her head.

> *It moved in circles, and I can only describe it as a bee buzzing. Then it seemed to have a man's voice, and it kept buzzing over and over, "I love you! I love you!"*
>
> *Whenever I turned the light on, it would go away. The second I snapped the lamp off, it would be back buzzing around my head.*
>
> *A few nights later, I had the sensation of someone getting into bed with me, and I heard the sound of breathing beside me. It smelled like rotton seaweed, and I was so frightened that I could not move. The next day the bed was wet on that side.*

Norma S. is often required to travel away from home in her job with the state board of health. One night in 1970 she lay in a clean motel room, dozing contentedly, when she felt someone get into bed with her. She stated her account of the incident:

> *I was in light sleep, I forgot where I was for a moment and thought that I was at home and my husband was crawling in beside me. Then I suddenly remembered my strange surroundings. I jumped from the bed and turned on the light. I was prepared to emit a scream that would have brought the National Guard down on whoever had slipped into my bed, but the sounds died in my throat. There was no one in my bed. I was quite alone.*

Norma went to the bathroom, got a drink of water, and decided that she had dreamed the whole thing. She chuckled softly to herself, thought about what a story it would be to tell her husband, then fell instantly asleep. She continued:

> When I awoke the next morning I stretched contentedly until, to my surprise and horror, I realized that a body was pressed full-length against mine. I lay shocked, frozen into immobility. Whoever lay beside me turned over, sighed noisily, and pressed a thigh familiarly against my own. I heard a male voice, muffled in the covers, say, "Oh how tiresome it gets traveling around the country."
>
> At last panic grabbed me. I leaped from the bed and grabbed for a chair, which I would willingly have smashed against any intruder—had any intruder been there. Once again my bed was empty, but this time the pillow next to mine clearly showed the indentation of a head resting on it!

Norma testified that although she usually likes to take her time getting dressed in the morning, she left that motel room in record speed.

To say that love and psychic ability may often cofunction or that the psychodynamics of one may trigger the other is not to claim that such a thesis can explain the wonder of either gift. This book is but another of my efforts to further explore and to more completely understand the powers that are humankind's very own.

"To say that love is an 'exchange of psychic energy' is to state a literal fact," Dr. Smiley Blanton declares in his *Love or Perish*. "The woman who scans the face of her lover anxiously when he is disturbed and reaches out with a soothing hand to comfort him is actually transmitting to him a healing force within her own nature. She is obeying the same kind of impulse that directs the heart to pump more blood to the wounded limb."

Such a wondrous exchange of energies through the Love Force constitutes the greatest gift that the Divinity can give us. Since the Divinity is, itself, Love, then the greatest thing that we can offer to the Divinity is an act of love to our fellow humans and to all other life forms on this planet and in the universe. The gift of love gives of ourselves and carries with it all those things of our spiritual essence that are most noble.

"Love is the crowning grace of humanity, the holiest right of the soul, the golden link which binds us to duty and truth, the redeeming principle that chiefly reconciles the heart of life and is prophetic of eternal good," Petrarch wrote in his fourteenth-century Italy. The passing decades have not dimmed the validity of his insight. The Love Force does indeed comprise the "crowning grace of humanity."

In the chapters that follow, I not only share provocative case histories, but I provide you with a number of exercises and techniques by which you might lay your own claim on the "holiest right of the soul," the Love Force.

2
LOVE AND SEX IN THE PSYCHIC WORLD

The Love Force flows so strongly between my wife, Frances, and myself that I find it almost impossible to be separated from her for even an overnight trip.

Although I telephone her several times a day whenever I must be away on business, Fran's psi abilities are so developed that I feel as though her "psychic eyes" are always upon me. Usually she tells me where I am, who I am with, and what I am doing before I can inform her of those specifics from my end of the phone line. Invariably, Fran provides me with a precise description of the person with whom I am discussing business or of particular people who may be attending my seminar.

I am, I assure you, a faithful husband; but I am certain that you will agree that having a wife with such incredible psychic abilities guarantees fidelity.

The aura of enchantment that Frances has spun around me grows ever stronger, and I feel in harmony with Madame Dudevant's (George Sand) sentiment that a man who is loved by a beautiful and virtuous woman carries with him a talisman that renders him invulnerable.

A good illustration of the manner in which the Love Force can crackle between us occurred when we were separated by a distance of more than a thousand miles while I was completing the last chapter of a book on which I had expended a great deal of energy. Fran knew how important this work was to me, and she had been giving me steady moral support over the telephone. The writing was going well, in spite of my loneliness. I kept up a steady pace at the typewriter knowing that when my assignment in the area was completed, I would be able to rejoin her.

The moment I typed the final work in the final chapter, I was startled by the ringing of the *outgoing* line of the WATS (Wide Area Telephone System) telephone. I knew this was impossible. The office that I was using was owned by a company that had installed only *outgoing* WATS lines. The wiring had been done by the Bell telephone company and had been designed to make *only* outgoing calls. It was impossible for an incoming call to be received on an outgoing line.

Impossible or not, the phone was ringing and the light was flashing its alert.

Before I could respond, the other two regular telephone lines began to ring and to flash simultaneously. I punched each of the three buttons in turn, and there was no one on any line—just dead silence.

Puzzled, I set the receiver down on its cradle, only to have all three lines begin to ring and to light up again. For an astonished several minutes, I sat and watched the telephone lines continue to become active in a sequence of three rings, silence, three rings, silence, and so on.

"I've got to tell Fran about this," I mumbled aloud in a confused whisper.

The telephone lines obliged me by quieting down long enough for me to call her long-distance. I told her first that I had finished the book and then that I was experiencing a very strange phenomenon.

"I think the energies are just trying to tell you that they are celebrating the completion of your book with you," she replied.

She may have been correct; after we had completed our conversation, the telephone lines stopped "celebrating" long enough for me to begin proofreading and polishing the manuscript of the last chapter.

The gentleman who was allowing me to use his office stopped by to see how I was doing, and I told him about the curious behavior of his telephone. He smiled indulgently and informed me that there was no way that the outgoing WATS line could be receptive to an incoming call.

As if in direct response to his confident denial of the phenomenon, all three telephone lines began to ring at once. Once again, each of the lines was dead to the receiver.

Frowning his bewilderment, he took advantage of a lull in the eerie activity and called the telephone company. They confidently repeated the assertion he had already stated to me: There was no way that his outgoing WATS line could ring in.

As he cradled the receiver, the WATS line rang.

"Well, that's very impressive," he chuckled, deciding to be entertained rather than confused. "Now let's see all three lines ring again—all at once!"

I think we were both surpised to see the lines and the lights obey him. He nodded his head in approval. "Let's see only the center line ring."

The two end lines stopped, and the center line continued flashing.

"That's remarkable," he said, "Now just the first line."

The first line complied.

"Excellent. Now let's see the WATS out-line ring in. I really want to see that again."

For the next several minutes, the three telephone lines followed his instructions to the letter. The phone was playing games with him. It seemed to have an intelligence of its own.

"Okay, Steiger," he said at last, growing tired of the demonstrations. "I'm going home now. Thanks a lot for haunting my office. Things will probably never be the same around here when you leave."

Thankfully, for the sake of my work schedule, the telephone seemed to have become weary of its sport also. The only call the rest of the day was from Fran, checking to see how things were going.

The fascinating displays of the unseen energies had not yet concluded, however. Later that same night, I became aware of a tapping at the window behind the desk where I sat polishing my manuscript. I turned around just in time to see a large black bird flying away.

I had shades of Edgar Allen Poe and his raven quoting, "Nevermore." This huge black bird, larger than any crow that I had ever seen, had been pecking at the window pane with its beak.

I felt compelled to call Fran at once and share with her an account of yet another weird visitation for the day.

I got her out of the shower, but she explained to me, as she patiently dried herself with a towel, that in many traditions the bird was a sign of a messenger from higher intelligences. She interpreted the manifestation as being yet another sign of approval for the book from multidimensional beings.

I accepted her explanation with a nice glow of pleasure, then cradled the receiver so that I could get back to work. Three minutes later, Fran called back to tell me that on the white throw rug beside the bed lay a long black feather, like no feather with which she was familiar.

We were separated by a thousand miles, but somehow a large black bird pecked at *my* window and dropped a feather at *Fran's* feet.

Today that same feather has a cherished place in my mementoes of a lifetime spent exploring the strange and the unknown. It is more than that, of course. It is also a tangible manifestation of the Love Force that flows between Frances and me.

In 1968 John Pendragon, one of England's leading clairvoyants, responded to a question I put to him:

> *There may be a relationship between sex and psychic phenomena. I believe that repressed sex can cause psychic phenomena. Psychics have much personal magnetism and a wide magnetic field. This often gives them a personality which some, not knowing otherwise, mistake for "sex appeal." It is just that something extra. Musicians often have it, and some artists, but as real sensitives are so few, I have not enough samples to determine whether they are generally more sexy than nonsensitives. It seems likely that they may be.*

To the late John Pendragon, the man whom many consider to be the most gifted seer of our time, it seems likely that those possessed of psychic gifts are generally more sexy than the nonsensitive. Pendragon resisted making a definite statement because of his lack of samples. It is not, of course, the task of the clairvoyant to go about collecting such samples and interviews. Such a task belongs to the writer-researcher.

"As soon as you start to give evidence that you have some ability to control psychic phenomena, many women want to get into bed with you," a talented professional psychic told me. "So many seem to think that whatever you've got can rub off on them."

I asked him how he dealt with the problem of having a clientele so eager to partake of his energies and talents by bedroom osmosis. "Brad," he sighed:

I simply tell them that for me, the physical plane scarcely exists. I tell them that I think of them all as my spiritual sisters. I see to it that I keep a spiritual Grand Canyon between these women and myself. I couldn't afford to start messing around this way, even if I weren't married.

Look, let's say, for the sake of discussion, that I weakened just one time—and some of these women who come to me for psychic guidance are damned attractive—and took one of my clients to bed. Could she keep her mouth closed about it? You bet your sweet crystal ball she could not! Other clients would get pouty, and pretty soon I'd have to service the whole flock of them.

And then you know the next step, don't you? Some smart reporter would get wind of it—and I tell you, there's always some reporter on my tail trying to trip me up, trying to find some way to "expose" me. I say, let them try. You know me; you've tested me and agreed that my talents are genuine. But let a reporter get wind of the juicy tidbit that I was taking my clients to bed, and I'd be plastered all over the front pages. Wire services would pick it up and blow it all out of proportion. "Psychic Has Love Cult! Psychic Conducts Satanic Sex Rites!"

Today, I have a hard time getting the newspapers to give me any publicity. *If I walked on water they'd bring in some skeptical scientists to prove that my bones were hollow and my feet were made of sponge rubber. If I astrally projected myself to the President's lap while he was making a televised speech to the* nation, and then disappeared again in full view of the cameras, the newspapers would give the story a single-column head and bury it in the want-ads.

But let them hear that I tickled a client's knee during a consultation, and the press would hold its own Inquisition and find me guilty of using my psychic talents as a cover for running a sex cult. No, Brad, my relationship with my clients is strictly professional!

A female medium told me that, as a young woman, she had been shocked to learn that so many of her male colleagues were homosexuals.

I'll never forget that time I walked into a seance parlor at one of our summer camps with the supposition that the room was empty! Two men for whom I had always had the utmost respect were engaged in fellatio. I gasped and ran from the room.

Later, one of the men, whom I had known for several years and had come to regard almost as a father, drew me aside and begged me to speak with him. He said that he was sorry that I had had to see him like that, but he told me that many years ago his spirit control had advised him never to marry. His control, who was a female entity, had warned him that she would leave him powerless if he took a living bride. His guide permitted him sexual release with men, however, and did not regard such liaisons as acts of infidelity.

I don't know if he was telling me the truth or not. But I'm a lot older now and less shocked by the world as it is.

Why are some male mediums homosexuals? I don't know. Maybe it has something to do with their extreme sensitivity and the fact that the very nature of their work causes them to withdraw from conventional society and to turn inward unto themselves. I've heard and read that there is a great deal of homosexuality among male dancers, actors, artists, and the like. Maybe these homosexual mediums aren't really so different in their psychological make-up from those performers.

"You might call me a throw-back to the holy man of old," a vigorous male medium told me. "If I know that I have an

> *important demonstration coming up, I'll abstain from all sexual relationships for as much as three weeks in advance. The more pent-up I am sexually, the better the phenomena seem to come."*

I asked him if he felt that there was a definite link between his sexual frustration and the production of psychic phenomena.

> *"Definitely," he agreed. "It's like the spirits, or whatever it is, feeds on all that dammed up sexual energy."*

Another medium, a female, disagreed violently with this point of view. She told me:

> *When one becomes involved in active spiritual work, one loses interest in sex. The development of the spiritual side of man simply reduces his desire, and if he should then force himself to indulge in sex, it would reduce his spiritual strength. I divorced my husband because I became convinced that his sexual demands on my body were sapping my spiritual strength. I have not had sexual intercourse in fifteen years, and everyone in this camp can testify to my strong control over phenomena.*

One of the nation's leading mediums agrees that there is a definite relationship between sexual expression and the functioning of one's psychic or mediumistic abilities.

"Mediumistic phenomena are most certainly related to sex," she said. "Many mediums, unfortunately, become sexual deviates from frustration, mental disturbances, and, perhaps, from the constant need to sublimate the enormous amount of psychic energy that constantly bombards them."

Another psychic counselor expressed yet another viewpoint.

> *I must have good sex expression if my psychic and mediumistic abilities are to function properly. Thank God, my husband, an excellent medium, shares this philosophy. We make it a practice to "warm" each other up before a psychic session and to "regenerate" each other after a seance or an extensive period of consultation.*

When we are at home, we may do this conveniently. However, at summer camp, when we are called upon to give readings or seances in the afternoon as well as in the evening, it becomes rather obvious to the others what we are doing in our cabin immediately before and after each session.

"Hey, don't go in there," we once heard someone call to a party who was about to knock on our door. "They're busy recharging each other's batteries!"

A well-known trance medium told me how her first marriage had ended in divorce because of her husband's inability to cope with the manifestations that haunted their marriage bed. "My husband worked hard during the day and needed his rest at night," she recalled. "Those pesky spirits seemed to realize this, and they would visit us nearly every night at bedtime."

The manifestations generally began with a tugging at the bedclothes. "Damn it!" the man would bellow. "Tell your devils to leave us alone."

As if they were mischievous children just waiting for such a reaction, they would seize the covers and tear them from the bed, leaving the couple bereft of their bedclothes. The medium told me:

On more than one occasion, my husband would get out of bed and grab his shotgun. There would actually be the sound of running footsteps, like they were afraid of him and were retreating from the room.

With a war cry, he would chase them down the stairs and out the door. Then, just when he thought he had them chased away, he would hear them thumping around back upstairs. Some nights the poor man would run up and down those stairs until he would just collapse exhausted into bed.

I used to live in mortal fear that one night one of the children would get up to get a drink of water and be shot down by accident by their father with his gun.

The greatest blow to me came when I returned home from work one night and discovered that he had burned all of my books and my personal notes relating to spiritual work. He considered

27

that such things were of the devil, and he hoped that he might rid the house of the "demons" by burning all my materials related to psychic matters. I was afraid for a while that he would decide to add the "witch" to the pyre as well.

That night the spirits were at him so bad that I knew that we would have to separate in order to protect his life.

What is it like being married to a man who may be the outstanding physical medium in the world today, a man who can control psychokinesis (mind over matter) to such a degree that he is literally a modern Merlin? I brought such a question to his wife of little more than a year. She said:

To answer that question best I'll have to start before our marriage, during our courtship.

On the nights when we had a date, the furniture would start dancing about the room anywhere from several minutes to several hours before his arrival. Drawers would open, sometimes just as I was about to reach for them. Other times they would close after I had removed the item that I had wanted.

I often thought that these manifestations must have occurred because he was visualizing me moving about in my apartment, getting ready for our date.

She told me that now, after marriage, the sensitive sometimes tunes in on her from her husband's office. She laughed:

It's like the apartment is psychically bugged. It is impossible to keep a secret from him. He has come home from the office and repeated, word for word, conversations that I have had with my girl friends.

Once I wrote a letter whose contents I did not want my husband to know about. It was an angry letter to a man who had begun to take advantage of my husband's good nature. Then I thought better of the whole thing and ripped the letter to shreds. When he returned from work that night, he told me precisely what I had written and expressed his pleasure that I had decided not to send the letter.

In 1919 Sarah Woodward married a rancher who lived in the Southwest. The rancher had been a widower for several years, much to the perturbation of his friends and their wives. He was a tall, ruggedly handsome man who owned a comfortable spread of grazing land. Matronly cupids in the area had been trying to play matchmaker for him for so long that they had almost given up on the eligible bachelor and stamped "not interested" across his forehead.

When he returned from a trip to St. Louis with his new bride, Sarah, the neighbors held a happy chivaree for them, and his friends' wives felt that once again all was right with the world. The women left the newlyweds alone, happily clucking about what a quiet, soft-spoken, and sensible woman Sarah appeared to be.

Sarah did, indeed, possess all of those virtues, but she also possessed a secret that she had not told even her husband. For several years before her marriage, Sarah Woodward had been a spirit medium.

Just a few months before she had met the tall handsome rancher, Sarah had decided to disavow her mediumship. She had found the physical and mental drain of mediumship to be too great for her rather frail constitution, and she had grown weary of watching the eligible men pass her by in favor of more orthodox mates.

Now, more than ever, Sarah thought, as her husband took her in his arms, she was glad that she had decided to keep her mediumship a secret. She would not have wanted to scare this man away, even though his rugged features made him appear that he would not be frightened by anything. But Sarah was soon to learn that her handsome rancher had also harbored a secret.

They were preparing to retire for the evening when Sarah was startled to see a woman walk unannounced into their bedroom. The woman stood motionless for a few moments, obviously seething with rage. Sarah looked at her husband, expecting him to speak of the woman, but he seemed to be unaware of her presence.

Sarah was admittedly unfamiliar with the local customs of the Southwest, but it seemed to her that invasion of privacy was rude no matter where one lived. This woman had no business storming into her bedroom, and Sarah decided to take it upon herself to tell her so.

"What do you want in this room?" Sarah demanded of the stranger. "All the guests have gone home!"

Her husband turned to her and laughed. "They sure have, and I guess you know we're still kind of on our honeymoon, aren't we?"

Sarah blushed. "We're not alone," she told her husband, who still remained oblivious to the woman's presence. The woman had put her hands on her hips and had begun to tap an angry foot on the hardwood floors.

Her husband turned around in surprise. "I don't see anyone. What are you talking about, Sarah?"

It was true, Sarah realized at last. Her husband could not see the woman; she was in spirit.

Sarah had time only to shout a warning before the angry, uninvited visitor from the spirit plane hurled a vase at her husband's head. He fielded the heavy glass vase on his shoulder, and it crashed to the floor.

"Louise! Louise!" her husband wept. "Please stop!" The violent psychic storm abated, and "Louise" left the bedroom. The rancher knelt on the floor weeping.

"She has a nasty temper, doesn't she?" Sarah said at last.

"She warned me that would happen if I ever remarried," the rancher said. "I've known she was in the house. I've felt her presence off and on for these seven years since she died."

Sarah nodded. He did not have to tell her these things; she had already received strong psychic impressions that had told her everything, but it did him good to talk about it."

"Well," she said, "she's one redhead who really lives up to their reputation for angry outbursts."

As soon as she had spoken the words, Sarah regretted having opened her mouth. Her husband looked at her quizzically. "How did you know she had red hair? None of the women tonight would have told you about her—or did they?"

"No," Sarah admitted. "I . . ."

Her answer was cut off by her husband. "You acted from the very first as if you could see her. You were talking to someone in the room before the disturbance began. "Sarah," he demanded, "could you see her?"

"Yes," Sarah answered. "I could see her."

"But how? I've felt her sometimes. I heard her once or twice. But I've never seen her. How . . ." Her husband's hands made futile gestures in the air before him; then he fell silent.

"Darling," Sarah began. "I've always been able to see men and women like Louise. Ever since I was a little girl."

"You can see ghosts?" her husband asked. His voice sounded as if it had come from within a deep cavern.

"I can see men and women who are in spirit," Sarah replied. "A woman such as Louise has remained earthbound because of her possessive nature. She is strong and proud, and she was taken from you when she was young. What people call 'ghosts' are usually the restless spirits of those who died violent deaths and cannot adjust to their sudden change of condition; or, in some cases, they are men and women who are tied to the earth because of deeds left undone or because of earthly attractions that remain too strong."

Her husband leaned forward, cradled his head in trembling hands. She had not intended to say so much. She knelt and began to pick splinters of glass off the floor.

"Sarah," he spoke at last. "Can . . . can you *talk* to ghosts, too?"

She thought for several moments before she answered his question. "I am . . . I used to be what is called spirit medium. I had given all that up before I married you."

But you could see Louise?" he reminded her, bringing the full force of his red-rimmed eyes to bear on her.

Sarah had already considered this. Somehow she had known that the gift of mediumship could not be surrendered so easily. Somehow she had known that her renunciation of a talent nurtured within her psyche by external forces could not be accomplished in the same manner that one resigns from an employment situation with which she has grown weary and uncomfortable. She would be a medium until whoever had blessed, or blighted, her with such gifts decided to withdraw them.

Her husband took her hands within his own and clasped them with his strong fingers. She knew what he was going to ask before he had found the courage to voice the words. "Could you . . . talk to Louise and ask her to leave us alone? I once loved her, but . . ."

He could no longer speak, but Sarah understood. He was a lonely man of flesh and blood who sought to make a new life for himself with a new bride.

Sarah walked the hallways of the ranchhouse that night, but she could neither see nor sense any sign of Louise. She searched every room in the sprawling house, but it soon became obvious to her that the angry spirit of Louise had spent its wrath for that night. Whatever unknown forces had given her the strength to remain within the walls of the ranchhouse had been at least temporarily dissipated by the violent manifestation in the bedroom.

Sarah told her husband that she was quite certain Louise would return again the next night when they prepared to go to bed. As an earthbound spirit, Louise felt most jealous about her husband's most intimate relationships, the ones she would least wish to have him share with another woman.

Certainly neither Sarah nor her husband felt like making love after such a vicious psychic attack. Louise had won the first round, and Sarah was convinced that the jealous spirit would return the following night to be certain that her husband would not enjoy conjugal privileges with a woman of material substance.

Sarah's prediction proved correct. As she and her husband were undressing, Sarah caught sight of Louise striding angrily into the room. The spirit shook an angry finger at the rancher. Sarah knew that the psychic fireworks were about to begin.

"Louise!" she shouted. "Listen to me!"

The spirit turned to her with a look of shocked surprise. "You shameless hussy!" Louise snapped. "How dare you speak to me? You come into my home like some common slut and try to take away my husband."

"He's *my* husband now," Sarah replied softly. The spirit had crossed the room and now stood eye to eye with her. Sarah could see the terrible hurt and angry churning behind the spirit's eyes.

"What do you mean, *your* husband!" Louise shrieked.

Sarah interrupted her. "Louise, you are in spirit! Stop, think; you know that you are no longer of flesh. Remember the day you died, the day they buried you?"

The spirit put its hands to its ears. "Stop it! Stop it! Or I'll scratch your eyes out!"

"This is no longer your home," Sarah went on, speaking in a soothing tone. "It is time for you to pass on. You should have moved on seven years ago. You need not worry about your husband. The concerns of the earth plane now mean nothing to you. Remember your loved ones with affection, but don't try to hang on to them. You must now be concerned only with things of the spirit."

Sarah continued to speak in a soft voice of Louise's passing, of her necessity to accept the world of spirit, until at last Louise dropped her hands from her ears. "That's why he has not touched me for these seven long years. It was so unlike him. He was always so affectionate. Then he just stopped touching me . . ."

The spirit turned to look sadly at the confused rancher, who sat on the edge of the bed. He had been in the process of pulling off a boot when Sarah had begun speaking. He still sat with a hand on his boot heel—frozen, immobile, fearful lest some movement, some small sound, might break the connection Sarah had established with the spirit world.

Louise began to weep. "I remember now," she said. "The minister standing over me. 'Ashes to ashes,' he said, and all my friends and relatives were standing there to agree.

"But I wouldn't believe it. I wasn't ready to leave. There was my husband, the ranch, the hard times I knew were coming. I had to stick by him and help him. These two old men came and said that they would guide me, but I told them to go to hell."

"Those men were your spirit helpers, your guardians," Sarah explained. "You should have gone with them. You should have realized that it was time for you to pass on."

"But I had to stay with my husband," Louise sobbed; then, the anger flaring again, "but he rewards me by bringing you home!"

Sarah put up a forefinger to hush Louise's outburst. "Remember, you have been in spirit for seven years. It is not good that man should live alone."

Louise scowled. "He had *me,* didn't he?"

But this time her anger could not last. Her image was beginning to waver. Realization of her actual state of existence was beginning to pervade her being.

"He had you while you were in your material body," Sarah said, "but now you are in spirit."

"Now I am in spirit," Louise echoed.

A brilliant glowing orb formed behind them, and Sarah could make out the forms of two men standing within the golden light.

"They're here again," Louise said. "The two men are here again."

"Are you ready to go with them this time?" Sarah asked her.

Louise nodded. "Be a good wife for him," she said.

Before Sarah could reply, Louise had stepped into the orb of golden, glowing light. Sarah caught a glimpse of two men with white beards, of a landscape of rich green grasses and multicolored flowers, and then there was nothing before her but her husband on the edge of the bed, still holding on to his boot heel.

The medium whom I have called Sarah eventually reentered the spiritualist ministry with the blessing of her rancher husband. When she told me her story in 1969, she was in her late seventies and living in a nursing home in California—still alert, still studying, writing down experiences taken from a lifetime spent on the threshold between two worlds.

THE SWORD OF DIVINE FIRE

Shortly before his death, a master metaphysician shared this mental ritual of protection with me. It was his belief that one should begin each session of psychic development or spiritual exploration with such an exercise. You may wish to begin your own experiments by brandishing the Sword of Divine Fire.

Visualize that you hold within your hands a great, double-edged broad sword that is alive with golden flames. See yourself extending the sword before you and begin to make a circle around yourself with its tip.

Wherever the sword goes, it leaves a glowing spot of flame—so that when you have moved the sword completely around you, you have surrounded yourself with a golden, magic circle of fire.

This circle will never leave, but if for any reason you believe it to be waning, simply repeat the process. If you feel yourself in special danger or are upset or discouraged, you may wish to reinforce the golden circle.

You have but to *ask* to see the golden flames surrounding you when you need reassurance that you are always being protected; but if the act of reinforcement serves in any way to comfort you, then by all means replicate the process as often as you wish.

The moment that you have first completed fashioning your golden circle of flame around your body, spread your arms and your legs and visualize that circular area as being completely filled with golden light. Imagine this to be your own mental and spiritual kingdom. You are the lord or the lady of this psychic province.

Visualize now a golden line of infinity, issuing from the top of your head, your crown chakra, to All-That-Is, God.

This is your lifeline to the Source, rather than to the world. Know that this lifeline will hold you upright when you are tired or feeling depressed or discouraged.

Visualize the lifeline growing taut, then feel your head go proudly upward, your spine stiffen resolutely. You are connected to the God-Force.

Next visualize another line projecting from your diaphragm, or waist, to the horizon. This is the other lifeline that links you to God's infinity.

As you breathe deeply of the highly charged oxygen that surrounds you in your golden circle of flame, you will be sustained and supported. You will feel the presence of All-That-Is around you. You will never feel alone again, for you understand that always with you in your golden circle of flame is the invisible presence of the Source.

From the first moment that you surround yourself with the golden circle from the tip of the Sword of the Divine Fire, you know that your life will be different.

Whenever you are feeling tired or upset, give a little tug to your lifeline, and you will receive a charge of energy almost instantly.

From the moment that you have fashioned the circle around you, you will find that your ability to develop remarkable ESP abilities has increased a thousandfold.

Astonishing opportunities in your life will present themselves to you.

You will find that your spirit rises above petty annoyances and that you are beginning to concentrate only on matters that affect the divine essence of you—your soul.

THE ETERNAL FLAME OF ISIS

As an added preparatory exercise to your ESP experiments, I offer a ritual that is said to be a portion of the mystic rites practiced in the ancient Egyptian temples of Isis and Osiris. It is believed by many metaphysical scholars that the human psychic centers may be stimulated by such a ritual to produce effects on the body and the brain. Try it. It may be the stimulus you have been seeking:

O Eternal Flame, symbol of purity and creative life, I invoke the flood of the creative power now to make manifest the conditions described in the words now being consigned to the living flame.

The word is now made flesh, and I confide the hidden, secret desires of my mind, heart, and soul to the creative spirit of the universe. All obstacles are now being removed; dust to dust, ashes to ashes; the invisible spirit released by these creative words now assumes individual identity and finds its fulfillment.

The words and thoughts now released from the burden of the physical and material world now reach the subjective mind of the Subjective Mind of the Universe and become objectified. Flame, creative life, return to the source of thy origin, and manifest as creative spirit that which is entrusted to thee.

I express faith in the power that rules time and space, that these conditions will be fulfilled. It is done, and I give thanks, O Eternal Spirit, ruler of the universe.

Serious practitioners urge that you implement the invocation by writing on a piece of paper your desires and wishes, then setting fire to them in a small dish or before an altar with two lighted candles. As you watch the paper burn, recite the invocation with feeling and faith. As the paper crinkles into ashes, visualize all obstacles to your wishes dissolving. As the smoke circles toward the ceiling, visualize the Eternal Spirit working in invisible ways to manifest the conditions that you have asked for.

A tip: So often those men and women who are just beginning to develop their ESP abilities (or who are working with altered states of consciousness) expect to *see* clear and distinct images at once.

Sometimes, especially when you are just developing, you will *feel*, rather than see something. You will seem to *feel* that something will occur at six o'clock. You will *feel* that it is your aunt who is trying to contact you. You will *feel* that you should not board that particular airplane and take that particular flight.

Seeing often comes later, after your psychic muscles have become better developed.

BE YOUR OWN PROPHET

My wife, Frances Paschal Steiger, claims that you don't need to go to a fortune teller to learn the answers to questions that trouble you. You can learn how to become your own prophet and to make your own predictions.

"Nature gave humankind an edge in the survival game by giving us a more highly developed psychic ability to combine with our intellectual brain processes," states Frances. "But for too many people, the ESP ability has come to be little used, like an undeveloped muscle."

Here is an exercise that Fran recommends to strengthen your prophetic muscles:

Get a notebook in which to keep score of your ability to predict according to your intellectual, rational level, and according to your hunches—your instinctual, psychic level.

Draw two columns on a sheet of paper, labeling one column "Intellect" the other, "Hunches."

Sit, lie, or assume a meditative posture of complete relaxation. Use your mental processess to come to a conclusion about the following future possibilities:

1. Seeing or hearing from a person from whom you have not had contact for a long period of time.
2. What color or what outfit someone you see regularly will wear at home, at the office, or on a date.
3. Two events that will occur at your home or your place of work—one negative, the other positive.

Write these thought-predictions under your "Intellect" column.

Now, permit yourself to enter an altered state of awareness as completely as possible. Clear your brain of all distractions. Imagine before you a blank white screen and permit images to form:

1. Imagine a person you will soon see or hear from with whom you have not had contact for a long period of time.
2. Imagine your date, friend, co-worker, or mate—what will that person be wearing when you next see him or her.

3. Imagine two events that will occur at your home or place of work—one negative, the other positive.

Record these meditative image predictions under your "Hunches" column and give both columns one week to be fulfilled.

Remember also to record events that come to you in dreams; predictive images often surface in the altered state of consciousness known as sleep.

At the end of a week, mark the outcome of the number of foreseen events that came true. See if you predict better by hunch or by reliance on your intellectual processes. If both columns correlate to a large degree, you have probably developed an excellent bridge between your psychic and your mental abilities.

Another method that may be used in conjunction with this exercise is using a newspaper as a tool to improve your psychic abilities.

1. Note the major political events in the newspaper. Attempt to predict their outcomes by both the "Hunch" and the "Intellect" methods.

2. Try to predict by both methods the subject matter and the exact words used in tomorrow's headlines.

3. Seek to tune in on who will be in the pictures in tomorrow's paper—men, women, children, celebrities—and envision what they will be doing.

You may wish to conduct these exercises with a friend or relative so that the two of you may cross-check one another. Continue these techniques for a month. The serious student will keep a running diary in order to obtain the most desirable results.

According to Frances, "These techniques can strengthen your ESP muscles and not only enable you to envision the future, but allow you to become a more complete and balanced person in everything you do."

"READING" OBJECTS

The famous psychometrist Dorothy Spence Lauer once shared the following exercise for encouraging the ability to "read" objects, which means to receive and share impressions.

When you first begin to psychometrize an article, such as a hairpin, letter, or earring, speak spontaneously. Do not hesitate to say exactly what comes to your mind.

There is no need to concentrate, or even to think hard; in fact, the secret lies in just being spontaneous, immediately saying what comes to you. This can be a little embarrassing, if something of a very intimate nature should come to you, but if you truly feel the urge to speak frankly, you should do so.

You may begin by psychometrizing for yourself. Take an object that belongs to you, something that you have worn or used for some time, such as a comb or a ring.

Sit quietly, holding the object. Do not force ideas or concentrate.

Have a pad and pencil at your side, and as fast as your thoughts come to you, write them down. There will be times when you will say, "This sounds impossible"; still, write it all down. Do not continue this exercise for too long a period, however.

By psychometrizing for yourself, you will find that you have received insights that can guide you in your daily life. Infinite intelligence can channel through you at this time.

Do not take credit for this information or become egotistical in your work. Remember the words from the *Bible*: "I, of myself, can do nothing."

The power that guides you will disappear if you become smug and arrogant. You must remember that you are an instrument tuned to receive.

When you psychometrize for another person, you may tell them your impressions rather than jotting them down. To further experiment and to increase your psychometric abilities, ask friends to lend you their old letters from people whom you do not know. Request objects that they have received through family inheritances and the like. Remember that you are an instrument and permit the messages to flow through you in a spontaneous manner.

Understand that there will always be a *knowing*. You will not guess. You will not waver. Never doubt your impressions once you learn to distinguish the sensations of the *knowing*.

Psychometry can be a great aid in business and in personal relationships. Suppose you are about to employ someone. Ask to hold a small article of his in your hand (not telling him why) and follow the impression you receive.

Arrogance in a prospective employee (or lover) is denoted by the object feeling warm in your hand. Greed is denoted by a feeling of nausea. This person would step over others for personal gain. A cool feeling will tell you that the person will do his best to make a successful business or personal relationship.

3

DREAM POWER AND DREAM LOVERS

Gloria F. could remember her dream in sharp detail the next morning when she awakened:

Her boyfriend, Roger, had asked her to go riding with him across the Illinois state line into Indiana. As they drove along the highway, they had collided with another car, and both vehicles sustained great damage. Through drops of blood blurring her vision, Gloria had watched a plump woman with her arm bandaged and in a sling crawl out of the other car.

With the dream images firmly implanted in her mind, Gloria refused Roger's offer of an automobile ride on that beautiful Sunday afternoon in May of 1971. "Come on," he coaxed. "Let's buzz over to Hammond and see if Indiana is as pretty as Illinois is today."

Gloria shook her head and told Roger about the dream that she had had the night before.

"Are you going to let a silly dream interfere with an outing on a day like today?" He laughed. "There won't be any wreck with old Steady Hand at the wheel. I'll even get you home early. Is it okay, Mrs. F?" he asked Gloria's mother, who was sitting on the porch swing reading the Sunday paper.

"I think an automobile ride would be pleasant on such a nice day," she answered, looking up from the recipe she was studying on the women's page. "Why don't you kids run along?"

Reluctantly, Gloria followed the triumphantly grinning Roger to his car. "Well, you drive carefully, Roger!"

And Roger did drive carefully, a point he was to emphasize repeatedly, until, halfway between Gary and Hammond, Indiana, they crashed into another car.

Gloria's head went through the windshield, and she staggered from Roger's automobile, wiping the blood out of her eyes. Dimly, she saw the driver of the other car removing himself from behind the wheel with great effort. The driver's wife, a very plump woman, was tugging at him with one good arm. Her other arm was bandaged and in a sling.

"If only I had followed the warning in my dream instead of listening to Mom and Roger," Gloria kept saying to herself as she sat in the doctor's office, waiting to have her skull stitched closed.

The enigma of the precognitive dream has long fascinated humankind and has, from time to time, received scientific attention in "dream labs" established in various universities and hospitals.

It seems that some level of the unconscious mind may well be aware of the future and that it may occasionally flash a dramatic bit or scene to the conscious mind in a dream or a trance, both of which are altered states of consciousness.

Psychical researcher H. F. Saltmarsh theorized that what we normally think of as the "present moment" is not a point of time, but a small time interval called the *specious present*. According to Saltmarsh's theory, our unconscious minds may be able to encompass a larger specious present than our conscious level of being. If, on occasion, some of this unconscious knowledge were to burst into the conscious, it might be interpreted as either a memory of a past event or a precognition of a future event.

We know that those events that we term our past are neatly cataloged somewhere in our unconscious. Some psychical researchers, including Saltmarsh, believe that all events—past, present, and future—are part of the "present," an eternal now, for the deeper, transcendental level of the unconscious.

The telepathic dream received a great deal of attention through the scientific inquiry of the Dream Laboratory at the Maimonides Medical Center in Brooklyn, New York. The experiments undertaken by the Dream Lab were designed to test the hypothesis that the altered state of consciousness associated with dreaming favors the appearance in the dream of a telepathically received stimulus. Eight experimental studies conducted by the laboratory between 1964 and 1969 produced five studies with statistically significant results.

In addition to the formal experimental studies, a number of pilot sessions were undertaken with equally rigid precautions against any kind of sensory leakage. Between March 25, 1964, and December 19, 1969, eighty-three pilot sessions involving one or more agents (senders) and a single sleeping subject (receiver) had been completed by the Dream Lab.

In a report prepared for the 1970 meeting of the Association for the Psychophysiological Study of Sleep in Santa Fe, New Mexico, Montague Ullman, Stanley Krippner, and Charles Honorton of the Maimonides Medical Center state:

> *For these pilot sessions, judging of correspondences between the randomly selected target and dream content was accomplished by presenting outside judges with the entire target pool for that night and asking them to assign the rank of number one to that target picture which most closely resembled [the subject's] dreams and associational material. The other targets were also ranked on a similar basis. If the actual target was given a rank within the top half of the distribution (e.g., number one or number two of a four-target pool), the rank was considered a "hit," supporting the telepathy hypothesis.*
>
> *For the eighty-three pilot telepathy sessions completed by the end of 1969, the judges assigned sixty-four "hits" and nineteen "misses." This distribution is statistically significant . . . . Of these eighty-three sessions, eleven were held with a relative (father, mother, spouse, sibling) serving as [agent], rather than a Dream Laboratory staff member. For these sessions there are nine "hits" and two "misses."*

The latter point is especially germane to the central thesis of this book: Paranormal phenomena function most efficiently and dramatically between agent and percipient who cherish strong emotional feelings toward one another and who flow together in the Love Force.

Consider the telepathic dream experienced by Gladys D. of Wyoming.

Because of severe drought conditions in the ranchlands, Gladys had taken a job in town in order to help out her family financially. During the summer she had commuted, but in the winter, because of the bad weather and the poor roads, she rented a small house in town while her husband and two sons stayed at the ranch.

At 3:00 on a January morning, the woman awakened with the acrid odor of burning cloth offending her nostrils. Terrified by the thought that her house might be on fire, she got out of bed and checked the small home thoroughly.

Although she found no fire in the house, the feeling of danger persisted. She concluded that the fire must be in the home in which her husband and sons lay sleeping.

Gladys called the ranch, but no one answered. She insisted that the operator keep trying.

At last she heard the click of the receiver being lifted, and nearly simultaneously with his "hello" she heard her older son coughing.

"Are you all right, Billie?" she shouted into the receiver.

"Mom! Mom! The house is full of smoke!"

Gladys told her boy not to panic. "Go wake up Daddy and Jimmy. Find out where the smoke is coming from, put out the fire, and call me back!"

After an excruciatingly long thirty minutes, Gladys's husband called. The boys had placed their gloves on the wood box to dry out that evening when they had come in from chores. Sometime during the night a spark had popped out of the stove and had landed on one of the gloves. The gloves had smoldered until they had burst into flame. When they located the fire, the gloves had been completely burned and the wood in the box was just beginning to crackle into flame.

Gladys went back to bed, relieved that no real damage had been done to their home.

"But I know that if I had not had that strange dream and smelled smoke where there was none and called the ranch, my home would have burned to the ground with my three loved ones in it," she stated in her account of the telepathic dream.

Sometimes, it appears, a telepathic bond between a man and a woman is so strong that they can share dreams. Numerous couples report having had common dreams or having been able to awake with an awareness of what the other had been experiencing in the dream state.

A spirit medium told me of a dramatic dream scenario that he and his wife had shared.

> *My wife had gone to bed rather early that night, and she was already sound asleep when I decided to crawl beneath the covers. I doubt if I had been asleep more than a few moments when I became aware of my wife calling to me for help. Somehow I answered that call, and I crossed over into her dream.*
>
> *My wife was crouching in a dank cave, cowering before some hideous, beastlike creature. I was frightened when I saw the hulking monster slavering over Arlene, but a part of my mind reminded me that this was only a dream. So, with a courage found only in bottles and dreams, I charged the monster with both my fists flailing.*
>
> *It turned out to be a royal battle! I could feel my fists thud against his bulk, and his rough, scaly flesh soon made my knuckles bloody. And it landed some good ones on me, too. Once I felt its talons rip my cheek, and I know I must have cried out in pain. It seemed as though I might be winning, when I heard Arlene screaming behind me.*
>
> *I managed to look over my shoulder, and I was horrified to see that the damned thing had called reinforcements. One hideous brute was holding Arlene by the shoulders while another demon was ripping off her pajama bottoms. A quick glance at the creatures' lower bodies told me that they were emphatically male, and there was little question as to their designs on Arlene.*
>
> *Then—why I hadn't thought of it before I don't know—I called upon my spirit guide for some reinforcements of my own.*

> *Instantly, in answer to my mental summons, Brave Knife appeared with two other warriors, each of them brandishing heavy war clubs. The ensuing donnybrook would have done credit to any John Wayne western.*
>
> *After we had beaten off the grotesque "bad guys," I scooped the sobbing Arlene up in my arms. At that moment we awakened from our bizarre mutual dream.*
>
> *But the really eerie part is that we awakened in the middle of the bedroom with me holding Arlene just as I had been in the dream. Arlene's hair was disheveled, and the bottom of her pajamas were off. Arlene gasped and touched a finger gingerly to my cheek. Blood was trickling down over my chin from a deep scratch on my cheekbone. My pajamas were ripped in three places. And someone had turned all the bedroom lights on.*
>
> *Had we somehow made the dream become a pseudo-reality by acting out its weird and monstrous story line? Or had Arlene drawn us into a shadow world wherein grotesque night creatures dwell? I cannot really answer those questions, but I do know that in spite of strenuous housecleaning, the bottom half of Arlene's pajamas never have turned up.*

Claudia Christianson dreamed that she died, and it may have been only the intervention of her husband, who was having a similar dream, that prevented her dream from coming true.

> *I dreamed that I had been shot by a thief as I walked on the street. Police officers came running up, and they, in turn, shot the criminal, but that was all too late to do me any good. They stretched my body out on a park bench, and I suddenly found myself walking through unfamiliar hilly and barren country.*
>
> *I walked on and on, watching the light fade and the countryside grow darker. Deep blackness was closing in around me, when I heard my husband shouting in my ear, "Honey! Honey! Don't leave me!" I heard his words over and over again, like a needle stuck in the groove of a phonograph record.*
>
> *I wanted to move, yet I could not. I wanted to answer him, but no sound came from my throat. I no longer had any control over my body.*

> *Dimly, I became aware of my husband sitting up in bed, turning me over on my back. I felt just a trickle of life returning to my body. I found myself awake, my sleeping husband bent over me. I managed to pat his hand, and he settled back down in bed with a deep sigh. Through all of his exertions he had never awakened.*
>
> *I lay there for quite some time, cautiously trying all my logy limbs to see if they were all working once again. At last I drifted back into an uneasy sleep.*
>
> *When the alarm went off that next morning, I awakened to find my husband holding me close to him. He told me that he had dreamed that I was leaving him forever to walk into a strange, barren land. He could not follow me past a barrier, but he could stand at the border and call for me to return.*

Claudia told her husband of her dream of death, and they lay there for several minutes, marveling over the strange manner in which the dream states had been shared.

Gerald Christianson raised himself on an elbow, started to speak, then stopped—a ghastly pallor draining his features of their normally ruddy hue. He reached to the bedside table and handed his wife a mirror. Claudia stated:

> *One look shocked me. The skin under my eyes, around my mouth, and at the edge of my nostrils was blue. It felt cold and lifeless. My fingernails were blue, and so were my toenails and the palms of my hands. My whole body was still rather unmanageable. My husband noticed a place in my eye where the white seemed to have congealed.*
>
> *The blue left my fingernails and my palms, and I regained the use of my body after a few hours, but it took a week for the blue of my face to go away. I still have the spot in my eye. Once when a doctor saw it, he said that I must have been very close to death at some time for such a spot to have formed.*

According to dream researchers, thousands of mothers-to-be have dreams of giving birth to grotesque demons and hideous monsters.

Dr. Stanley Krippner, who served as the director of the William C. Menninger Dream Laboratory at Maimonides Medical

Center in Brooklyn, New York, said: "We have found a large percentage of pregnant women who dream about giving birth to deformed babies and monsters. These dreams express a natural fear that something will go wrong with the unborn child. So many mothers have these dreams that we do not consider them to be pathological in most cases."

In research conducted by Diane R. Schneider, with the co-sponsorship of Dr. William Pomcranre, director of the Maimonides Hospital obstetrics department, it was determined that pregnancy, the wish for pregnancy, and the fear of pregnancy actually influence dream content to a high degree.

Dr. R. L. Van de Castle, research consultant to Ms. Schneider's project, noted that occasionally a woman may have a dream that accurately foresees the future in regard to her pregnancy and her delivery.

Dr. Van de Castle discovered one woman who claimed that she had had recurring nightmares for several years, ever since the time she had seen illustrations of an abnormal fetus in her fiance's medical textbook.

The woman said that her dreams were always identical. She lay in a hospital bed in hard labor. Her sister was always in the dream, and she, too, was in the last stages of pregnancy. The dream always ended the same way. Her sister gave birth to a healthy, normal child, and the dreamer, after long, excruciating labor, bore a deformed baby.

The woman suffered through the dreams for nearly six years before she married and became pregnant for the first time.

"Then I knew instinctively and absolutely that the pregnancy would repeat itself identically with the dream," she told Dr. Van de Castle. "And it did, even to my sister actually being pregnant at the same time that I was."

As in the recurring dream, the woman's sister gave birth to a healthy, normal girl, while she bore a deformed stillborn child.

When the woman became pregnant again a year later, her doctor warned her to expect a psychologically difficult pregnancy because of her previous experience.

"But I assured him that now the dream had lived itself out in reality; there would be no more worry on my part," the woman said. "The dream never recurred, and I gave birth to a normal child."

Megan J.'s precognitive dream had a happier message, and

because the young woman believed in its declaration, she saved the life of her unborn child.

Megan was in her second month of pregnancy when her doctor advised her that she must have an abortion. In his opinion, it would be fatal for her to bear the child. At her husband's urging, the woman made the necessary arrangements.

Then, the night before the operation, she had a dream in which an angel appeared before her holding a handsome baby boy in his arms. On the strength of that dream, Mrs. J. refused the abortion and carried the baby full term. Seven months later, she gave birth to the smiling baby boy she had seen so vividly in her dream.

When Evelyn R. was pregnant, she and her husband lived with in-laws, and she charitably described their arrangement as "an unhappy situation." Whenever she had had a particularly trying day, Evelyn would experience the same beautiful dream in which she was walking among lovely flowers with a little girl at her side and soothing, uplifting music playing in the background.

After her little girl was born and they had moved into a home of their own, the beautiful dream ceased, but Evelyn often thought of it.

When her daughter was about five, she took the girl along to a flower show that was being held at a convention hall in a nearby city. The entire hall had been transformed into a lovely, fragrant garden, and an orchestra played soothing, uplifting music.

"Suddenly it struck me," Evelyn wrote in her report of the paranormal experience. "This was my dream, that beautiful tension-relieving dream that I had had when I was pregnant!"

The most remarkable facet of this particular report occurred when Evelyn's daughter tugged at her skirt, her eyes sparkling excitedly, and said: *"We've* been here lots and lots of times before, haven't we, Mommy?"

Now we shall examine the assertion of certain men and women that they dreamed lovers who came true.

For centuries love ballads have sung of our desires for dream lovers to call our own. Memorable lines of lyric poetry have promised lovers from the theatre of the mind that would one day materialize as consorts of flesh and blood.

Is it possible that a seed of love planted in a dream can someday produce a mature and lasting relationship?

Maureen Connors answers in the affirmative.

"My dream lover and I actually grew up together," she told me. "I first dreamt about Todd when I was around five or six. I swear it. I was that young."

According to Maureen, she would always dream of the same place, a lovely cottage near a sandy stretch of beach. And there, playing near the waters of magnificent expanse of ocean, was a blond-haired, blue-eyed little boy of her own age.

"Right away, people who knew anything about me would start to laugh at this point," Maureen smiled, shaking her long dark hair to emphasize her acceptance of the skeptical mind. "After all, I grew up in Kansas, far away from any ocean. And I am very dark complexioned with brown eyes. So I can just hear the cynics commenting about childish fantasies of a terrain and a playmate that would be my opposite."

But the dreams of the boy, whom she knew was named Todd, persisted all through high school.

"I would dream about him at least once a month," she said. "We literally did grow up together. We got taller. We filled out. And when I—I should say, we—were sixteen, Todd's parents moved from the neat house by the beach to a large city. I should also mention that I had also seen his parents, and when his younger brother came, I knew him, too."

Although she was dating rather seriously when she graduated from high school in 1972, Maureen knew that a permanent relationship with any male other than Todd was really out of the question.

"By then, I had come to believe with every fiber of my being that Todd was to be my destiny," Maureen stated.

"I just totally accepted the fact that one day we would really meet in person and that we would be married."

A child of the 1960s, Maureen had longed to participate in significant peace marches while she was in high school. However, teenaged hippies were something of a rarity in small Kansas towns, especially if they came from good middle-class families and had to be home by midnight.

"Although it was true that my protests were mainly composed

of wearing jeans with the knees out and leather vests with Indian beads, I had developed a growing social conscience. I went to college planning to enter either law or social work."

Dreams of Todd went with Maureen to college, but it wasn't until her first year of graduate school that she actually met him.

"On a beautiful October afternoon in 1976, Todd and I almost collided with one another in the stacks at the Northwestern University library," Maureen laughed.

"It was incredible. He was just as I had seen him in my dreams. His mouth dropped open when I spoke to him by name. My heart was beating so fast that I really thought that I would faint. I think his name came out like the croak of a big bird."

Todd looked at the stranger who had just appeared before him and who had just dropped all the books that she had been cradling in her arms. He frowned, asked how she knew his name, then said very softly: "I don't know your name, but I know you from *somewhere*. Didn't we go to school together when we were kids? Back in California, I mean?"

Todd had been born in Santa Monica, and his family had lived there until his father was transferred to Chicago in 1970.

Maureen acted quickly and invited Todd for a cup of coffee.

"He was about to become engaged when we met, but I wasn't about to let anything come between us now that I actually had him before me in the flesh. I didn't *immediately* come right out and tell him about our dream relationship. I think I waited until he was on his third cup of coffee. Thank God, he didn't laugh. I really think I might have punched him out if he had laughed."

Todd did think for a while he had met a true "Dorothy" from Kansas who spoke to the Wizard of Oz on an intimate basis, but he heard Maureen out, then asked her to a movie that night.

"I really believe that for the longest time Todd thought that I had come up with the most original line that he had ever heard to get to meet someone," Maureen smiled contentedly. "But now, after seven years of marriage and two kids, it really doesn't matter."

A case worker for the welfare department in Cook County, Illinois, Maureen exercises her concern for social issues while Todd teaches American literature on the secondary level. As a post script, she added:

"Each morning I begin the day by asking my two girls, aged four and two, if they have had any good dreams while they slept.

I'm starting right now to monitor their dream lives. I am curious to see if any of this can be transmitted genetically."

Dom Spicuzza had never been out of the Bronx when Uncle Sam shipped him to Vietnam.

"I went right from the old neighborhood to boot camp to 'Nam before I could even learn how to spell 'Viet Cong,'" Dom wrote in his account of his dream lover who came true.

"The only thing that gave me any stability at all in those terrible days was my dream of this pretty little girl who lived in the country somewhere. I mean, she looked like a milkmaid in a dairy commercial on television. Every time I dreamt of her, I would wake up feeling like that country song about the guy yearning for the green, green grass of home."

Although Dom's life was subways, crowded streets, a crammed apartment with a widowed father and four brothers, he had his stormy adolescent years pacified by a dream of walking through a picturesque covered bridge on a bright spring day in the country. He would stroll happily beside the creek until he came to an old stone farmhouse. Dimly aware of someone at his side, he would enter the home and find himself in the utilitarian kitchen where a lovely young girl with light brown hair would be stirring some kind of batter in a bowl.

The girl would always look up at him with great affection and warmth in her large green eyes. And because it was a dream, she would walk right into Dom's outstretched arms.

"It was like we had known each other for years," Dom wrote. "I would call her by name—though I could never remember it in the morning—and we would hug and hold each other like we would never let go."

The dream became a talisman for Dom. "It got me through some pretty rough times. I was always kind of shy with the girls, and I really went through a bad scene with pimples and acne and all those teenaged curses. It never hurt quite as much when the girls teased me or avoided me, because I knew that somewhere this fantastic little lady was waiting for me."

After the adolescent blights had left him, Dom admitted that he did not seek to lead a monklike existence. He dated, even had a steady girl for a while.

"But at the weirdest and sometimes most disadvantageous

moments, I would start thinking about that beautiful chick in the country kitchen that I knew was waiting for me somewhere."

It was while Dom was in Vietnam that he had a particularly memorable dream. He had been drinking far too much while on an rest and relaxation weekend with some buddies. He was trying his best to sleep through a hangover when he saw the wholesome young country girl so clearly that he almost thought she was there with him in that two-bit hotel.

"She was shaking her finger at me," Dom recalled. "And she really looked disgusted. 'Listen, you dumb lug,' she said. 'I'm not going to wait for you forever. And I won't wait at all if you behave in such a disgusting manner. Look at you. You look and smell like a pig!'"

Dom cleaned up his act after the vivid dream and toned down his party-time activities.

Through the unfathomable process of logic so often associated with the military, Dom, who had barely known how to drive when he had entered the service, now found himself assigned to a motor pool. Reared by his father to always make the best of any situation in which he found himself, Dom resolved to learn as much as possible about the mechanical aspects of the motor vehicles in his charge and to focus on becoming a really good driver.

Upon his discharge in 1971, Dom got a job with a trucking firm that transported produce from the farm regions in upstate New York into the grocery stores of the Big Apple.

"I've learned that there really are no coincidences in life," Dom wrote, "but one day I got lost and found myself suddenly on a country road that looked very familiar. Pretty soon I knew that right around the next bend I would see the old covered bridge, the creek, and the stone farmhouse."

Within the next few moments, Dom was seeing it all—just as he had in his dreams so many times before. He did not, however, stride boldly into the kitchen. He did not wish to be arrested for breaking and entering or to be shot by a protective father—or worse, by a jealous husband.

"I prayed that I had not located her after all these years only to find her married to somebody else," Dom went on.

When he pulled his truck into the graveled farmyard, he was surprised to see a man with whom he had dealt at the vegetable market come out of the house to investigate his arrival. He knew the man only as Hugh, and he didn't know if the farmer would even recognize him.

"Whatsa matter, hey," the farmer teased him. "You lost or something?"

Dom admitted that he was, then asked if he might use the telephone to call his boss and explain why he would be late.

As Hugh walked beside him to the stone farmhouse, Dom remembered how in his dream there had always been someone near him as he had entered the home. Dom was so nervous that he felt as though he could not breathe.

In the next instant, he was inside the warm kitchen, and he was staring at the back of a girl with light brown hair who was stirring something in a large mixing bowl.

When she turned around to acknowledge the presence of a stranger in the house, Dom beheld the young woman of his dreams.

Suddenly, he remembered her name. "Linda," he nearly shouted his joy and amazement.

The large green eyes blinked, and the full lips worked at a quizzical smile in a manner that had become so familiar to Dom over the past nine years.

Hugh was edging between them. His fists had bunched, and he didn't look as hospitable as he had a few minutes ago.

"How did you know my sister's name?" the farmer demanded. "Have you ever met her?"

At the sound of the word "sister," a one-thousand-voice angelic choir sang a hallelujah.

"If he had said, 'wife,'" Dom confessed, "I probably would have got back in my truck and driven it off the nearest cliff."

Dom grinned at Hugh, "Linda means 'pretty' in Spanish. Your sister certainly is pretty. Right?"

The open smile and the quick-witted compliment won Dom an invitation to dinner.

"That was all the opening I needed," he said concluding his account. "Now I drive the truck from the country to the city, and Linda and I have a small truck garden next to Hugh's farm. This countryside had the green, green grass of my true home, and it had the green, green eyes of my true love."

Learning how to control your dreams cannot guarantee you a dream lover and his or her eventual physical materialization in your life, but such an ability to direct your internal dream theater can help you to focus the Love Force in a more productive manner.

Dreams of love and inspiration are best achieved by entering the Silence of meditation and altered states of consciousness with the proper goals held foremost. In the Silence the most holy of energies is concentrated.

When you enter the Great Silence, you will feel and know that it is composed of the vibrations of Cosmic Light and Love. You will sense around you the presence of great master teachers and highly evolved spiritual beings.

The essence of the Silence is the power of the light and unconditional love. And pulsating deep within such light and such love is the essence of the Source of All-That-Is, God.

SEEKING A DREAM OR VISION OF LOVE

Be still within and without, knowing that the Source is about to enter all levels of your consciousness and all levels of your being.

Take three comfortably deep breaths, holding each for the count of three. Feel at one with the essence of the Source that will blend with you.

Visualize a golden flame of love within your heart chakra, which is one of the seven energy centers of the body in Yogic and esoteric tradition. In your consciousness, travel a ray of golden light from your heart to the Source of All-That-Is that exists above you. Understand that, powerful and beautiful as the feeling of the Source is within you, your soul energy can absorb only an infinitesimal percentage of its true majesty. You must now send a beam of your essence to the Source that vibrates in a dimension above you.

Feel yourself becoming closer to the Source of All-That-Is. See points of violet light touching every cell of your physical body as your light begins to connect with the Love Force. Begin to sense strongly a closeness, an unity with the Source.

Concentrate for a moment on making your body as still as possible. Direct your attention to the Source and focus on the flame within your heart chakra. See clearly the ray of light that you are transmitting to the Source of All-That-Is.

Now feel your consciousness melding with the Love Force and begin to request a vision. Eliminate awareness of the physical body as much as it is possible for you to do so. Understand that your body is a connection to the Earth and nothing more.

Visualize yourself holding open hands to the Source, as if you were about to receive some object of a material substance from It. Mentally affirm the following:

"Source of All-That-Is, give unto me a dream that will charge me with love. Grant that the vision will show me all that I need to know for my good and for my gaining in my love relationships."

A tip: On the day when you plan to ask for a particularly meaningful dream, it is wisest to make a direct application for the experience immediately upon arising. Begin with your first consciousness and prayerful activity to make a positive affirmation that your dream will be achieved.

Then, from time to time throughout the day, quiet yourself, if even for a moment, and give recognition to the Source that exists both above and you within.

Visualize the Source as the eternally powerful energy that ignites the golden flame of love that burns within your own heart chakra. The more profoundly that you can visualize this connection, the greater the results of your vision.

Although we realize intellectually that the Source is an energy, it does aid us in achieving the transfer if we visualize It as an individualized presence.

Some still prefer the image of a loving father or mother. Others focus upon the image of a glowing light being.

Since we humans seem to communicate more effectively with images that most resemble us, I always encourage my students to develop a personal idea of loving intelligence that is ready to answer their every call, that is willing to grant every request that is for their good and their gaining.

It is truly important that you visualize and attempt to feel the reality of that individualized presence above you. Know that it is connected to you by a ray of light, a stream of love-energy that flows into your body through your Crown Chakra (top of your head).

Several times a day before seeking a profound vision, give your attention to your personal image of the Source and send your love to that holy presence. If you prefer, you may verbalize your love and call the name of your guide or teacher to aid you in intensifying the transmission. Many students have said they have actually felt a warmth touching the tops of their heads during their sending of love to the Source.

Just remember that the summoning of a dream or a vision must always be as the result of a balanced desire.

Great teachers tell us that the positive use of the love energy from the Source of All-That-Is is the greatest need of humankind today.

I have been advised by some that in sending love to the Source, one should visualize a pink, as well as golden, flame issuing from your heart chakra.

These teachers maintain that the combination of the pink and the golden flames truly constitute a key that will unlock the door to exceptionally meaningful dream teachings.

HOW TO RECALL A DREAM

There may be occasions when you will awaken in the night and know that you have been receiving dream teachings. You may feel distressed when you become aware that you have been unable to retain the full importance and meaning of the dream.

Call out to your guide to help you to recover the full understanding of that which the Source wishes you to know. Ask that you receive again the full power of the vision that has just been entrusted to you.

Do not permit yourself to become angry or frustrated with yourself for having permitted the great lesson to have become lost to your waking consciousness.

If you should not be able to recall the lesson on that particular evening, go back to sleep with the resolution that you shall reclaim it on the next night.

Prepare yourself during the day with the transmissions of love to the Source that I have just described. Then, before going to sleep, call upon the Love Force to send its mighty energy into your body.

Charge yourself to bring back the vital substance of the dream teachings that you shall receive anew.

Ask your guide to stand watch over you so that only good enters into your reception of the teachings.

DISSIPATING DISTURBING DREAMS

Even after you have developed dream control, you may, from time to time, receive disturbing dream images about certain individuals or about humankind in general. It is not good to harbor this vague, but often troublesome, dream residue.

When you arise and go about your daily tasks, visualize an aura of violet light around everyone you meet. Soon, only positive thoughts about all individuals will command your attention.

If you should awaken some evening and feel that you have been bombarded with negativity while your psyche was open to receive a dream of love or inspiration, deal with the chaotic energy in this manner:

Visualize your *head* filled with a glowing violet light. Imagine that your are focusing the energy of the Love Force through your brain.

Expand the violet light, the highest spiritual vibration, to shine beyond your bedroom. See it shining its love forth upon your neighborhood, your city, your nation, your world. Then visualize yourself suspended in space watching your love energy touching minds of the universe.

See that your *heart* has become a violet-colored star; then expand its light to fill the room, the neighborhood, the city, the nation, the world, until it touches the heart of the universe.

Now feel that your very body has turned into gold. The violet light of the Love Force has transmuted the lead of your body into the finest quality of gold.

As a golden one, hold now in your mind a request for the love dream that you feel that you most require for your good and your gaining. Continue to hold that request in your mind until you fall back asleep.

ATTAINING A VISION OF LOVE

Place yourself in a very restful, meditative state. Play some New Age music, such as Steven Halpern's *Starborn Suite* or Michael Stearn's *Ancient Leaves*.

Study the following procedure so that you may retain the

essence of its steps in order to guide your inner self to the vision. Or prerecord your voice, giving yourself step-by-step instructions from a cassette recorder.

Image yourself surrounded by a violet light. Feel the warmth of the light from the Love Force beginning to stimulate your crown chakra.

Become one with the feeling of being loved unconditionally by an intelligence who has always loved you—just as you are. Sense the presence of an intelligence that you have known was near to you ever since you were a child.

Be aware of a sensation of warmth in both your heart chakra and your crown chakra.

Be aware of a ray of light connecting your individual spirit essence to the higher vibration of the Love Force.

Image that the violet light has now acquired a tinge of pink. See it begin to swirl around you, moving faster and faster until it begins to acquire a form and a substance.

Visualize now the shape of a body . . . hair . . . a beautiful smile on a loving face. Become especially aware of the eyes. Feel the love, the unconditional love, that flows out to you from those eyes.

Take a moment to immerse yourself further in the warmth of unconditional love from this higher intelligence. Now be aware that materializing before you is the image of your angelic guide.

You have an inner knowing that your guide has come to take you to a special place where you will be able to receive a clear image of the one who will be your life partner in love, to better perceive the true nature of a current love relationship, or to achieve a better understanding of the power of the Love Force. Whatever it is that you most need to know about love for your fullest good and gaining will be revealed to you in this place.

Your guide stretches forth a firm but loving hand. Take that hand in your own.

Feel angelic love flowing through you. Feel the vibration of love from one who has always loved you, just as you are. Feel the vibration of love from one who has loved you with pure, heavenly, unconditional love. Feel the vibration of love from one who has come to take you to a special place where a profound vision of love awaits you.

See a violet mist clouding up around you as you begin to move through time and space with your angelic guide.

See yourself now in a holy place. You may be seeing yourself in a beautiful garden that lies before a majestic temple. You may be seeing yourself in a magic place in a forest. You may be seeing yourself high in some mountain retreat.

There is now a vibration in the air as if bells are chiming. At that sound, that signal, a wise teacher comes to meet you. (The teacher may be either male or female in form, whichever you prefer.) See the love in those eyes as the teacher sees you!

Look deeply in the eyes of that beloved teacher. As you do so, you learn the name of this great master teacher.

Become totally aware of this teacher. See his clothes, his body, his face, his eyes, his mouth, the way he holds his hands.

The teacher tells you that he has a gift of love for you. He says that it is a very special talisman that will help you in achieving a deep and powerful love experience.

He reaches within his robe and brings forth a leather bag. He opens the leather bag and hands you the gift.

Look at the gift. See what it is. Take the gift. Feel it. Know it. Tell the teacher how you feel about him and his gift.

Now you are once again aware that your angelic guide is beside you. Your guide has taken your hand to walk with you behind the master teacher.

You are now in a tunnel. The master teacher is leading you to a secret place.

Experience your emotions as you walk silently between your guide and your master teacher. Feel deeply your expectations. See the torches set into the walls.

Be aware of any aromas . . . any sounds . . . any sights.

Now you are in a great room. Look around you slowly. See statues and paintings arranged around the room—each one dedicated to the Love Force. See them and remember them.

The teacher is now showing you a great crystal that is supported on a golden tripod. He says that it is a great transmitter of the Love Force.

As you lean forward to stare into the crystal, the teacher tells you that he will now permit you to see the vision of love for which you have come to this dimension of awareness.

He tells you that you will now see all that you need to see at this time for your good and your gaining.

You will see all that is necessary for your present level of understanding.

You will see a vision of love that will be completely individualized for you and your particular needs.

See the vision . . . *now*!

When you return to full consciousness after the vision has been induced, hold the images in your mind as long as you can. It is important that you hold the thought-forms as long as possible so that you can impress their energy upon Earth plane reality.

The vision images of light and of love will open your desires so completely that they will soon condense into the patterns which you are visualizing. Sometimes you will feel a compulsion to share the message of your vision. Do so. In such a case, each time you share the vision with another person, you will receive even more details of the experience.

You will clearly know when a vision is intended only as individualized instruction for you and should not be described to another.

4

HEART-TO-HEART COMMUNICATION

When Elise V. experienced extreme feelings of uneasiness and nausea, she somehow knew that the sensations were related to her husband.

"Tony was at work," she said. "Although he had looked well when he left for his job, I knew that he was sick. It was as if I could actually hear him saying, 'Elise, please come and get me. I'm terribly sick.' And then waves of nausea would hit me."

Elise reached the point where she could no longer bear her uneasiness, and she changed her dress and drove to the factory where her husband worked. An inquiry at the desk produced the information that Tony was not at his job, but was in the dispensary. The nurse there had been trying unsuccessfully to reach her at home.

When Elise walked into the dispensary, she found her husband sitting down, extremely pale and in great pain. Two of his co-workers, who had helped him into the office, stood on either side, ready to assist again if need be. Elise accepted their offer to help her husband into the car.

"What made you come after me?" her husband asked, once she had him home and in bed.

"I don't really know," she admitted. "I felt I was just being silly, but I had a terrible feeling of uneasiness that you were sick and in pain."

"Well, you were right," he sighed. "You came just when I needed you. You amazed everyone when you came walking into the dispensary while the nurse was trying to call you at home."

On July 2, 1951, the Los Angeles *Daily Mirror* published an account of the accidental drowning of Thomas Wall. The twenty-five-year-old man had drowned in MacArthur Park Lake while scores of spectators had watched helplessly from the shore, less than 200 feet away. His companion, Joseph Cefalu, had managed to swim to shore after making a futile attempt to save Wall.

Frances Wall, the dead man's wife, arrived on the scene shortly after the body was recovered. A premonition that something had happened to Wall had brought her from home.

William H. Gilroy investigated the incident and obtained statements from Joseph Cefalu and Frances Wall. According to Cefalu, Tom Wall had stopped by his apartment and asked him to go to the park with him. They took a sunbath, then, at Wall's suggestion, rented a canoe. They had started across the lake when Wall suddenly became concerned about the time. He had promised his wife that he would take her to dinner and a show that night. For some reason, Cefalu stated, Wall had stood up in the canoe and they had capsized.

In Frances Wall's account, she told how she had declined Tom's suggestion to go to the park and sunbathe. During the early afternoon she had worked about the house, bathed, and put her hair up in curlers. She lay down to read and dozed off; then she was wide awake, hearing her husband's voice crying: "Frances, come to the park! I'm drowning!"

"His voice was as loud and distinct as though he were right in the room with me," she told Gilroy. "I sat there stunned and sick. Again his voice cried out, 'Frances, Frances, please hurry.'"

"I don't remember how or what I put on, but I found myself outside the apartment, running toward the park. Before I had traveled half the distance to the lake, I saw a crowd gathering near the shore, and I knew without going nearer that my Tommy had gone away from me forever.

"Much later, someone found me wandering about the streets and brought me home."

A student in an Eastern college, whom we shall call Edgar Morris, found out that it is possible to hurt the ones we love telepathically as well as emotionally.

Edgar had always been a high academic achiever, and by the time he was a sophomore, the word was out that Edgar raised the class curve on any examinations he took. For those students who were also academically oriented, Edgar Morris became *the* man to beat.

Then, near the close of his sophomore year, Edgar met Alice, and Cupid's deadly darts began to take their toll on his study time.

"The climax came after this big test in sociology," Edgar said. "When the grades were posted, I was shocked to see that I had barely received a passing mark. Some of the fellows in the class cheered, and nearly everyone was laughing at my humiliation. One of my rivals in the class passed me in the corridor and whispered: 'Every Samson has his Delilah!'"

Edgar Morris was not so academically aloof that he could not feel the pinch of terrible pride. He went to a campus coffee house with his closest friend and told him of his intention of breaking off with Alice.

"Hey, c'mon, man. You're throwing away a great chick like Alice because of a nick in your grades? You're unreal, baby," his friend said, shaking his head sadly.

"I'm serious," Edgar replied. "I cannot jeopardize my academic standing. Perhaps later we might be able to take up again. I hereby decree that as of this afternoon, at 3:55 P.M., Alice and I are no longer a 'thing.'"

Edgar bade his friend farewell and went back to his room to attack the books. Perhaps it was not too late to regain the precious points he had lost in his sociology class.

After two days had passed, Edgar began to notice that he had not seen Alice in the coffee house or in the one class they shared. When he inquired about her, he learned from one of her friends that Alice lay in a strange semi-coma at the campus health service.

According to her friend, Alice had been perfectly well until about four o'clock two days before. At that time, she had suddenly heaved a deep sigh and fainted. Neither the girls nor the campus doctor had been able to revive Alice for more than short periods of consciousness.

Edgar went directly to the health service and asked to see Alice. Although she seemed to be lying on her bed in a light trance state, she became immediately animated the moment Edgar walked into the room.

"You deceitful creep!" she screamed. "So I no longer mean anything to you! So you are going to leave me! You cruel . . . cruel . . . ."

"For a second there, " Edgar said, "Alice couldn't think of a word, and I couldn't think of anything to do. Then I walked over to her bed and kissed her and told her that she was all upset over nothing. Alice was out of the infirmary in a couple of days, and since that time I have been finding ways to budget my time so that neither Alice nor my studies are neglected."

Many of us have known couples who have grown so close over the years that it is difficult to visualize one of them without the other. It may well be that such couples form an enormously powerful telepathic bond that is responsible when we read that an elderly person has passed away, only to be followed in death a few days later by his or her mate. Not long ago I received an account where such a telepathic link-up may have been involved in the near-death of an elderly woman.

Russell C. had always been a powerful man, strong of body, mind and will. Although theirs had been a happy marriage, Anna C. had often been forced to bend to the desires of her indomitable husband.

At last, when he was nearly eighty, his powerful old frame began to weaken, and Russell was forced to become a virtual invalid. His fierce pride suffered, as he had never been ill a day in his life. His humiliation was all the greater because Anna, who had always been such a frail little woman, remained active and well.

Russell was, at last, taken to a hospital. His doctor realized that the old man was still dictating to his wife, and she was dutifully waiting on him hand and foot. Russell had been in the hospital about a week when, one night, I stopped by to visit Anna.

She had excused herself to put the coffeepot on, when she clutched for her throat and buckled at the knees. I ran to her side, fearing that she had suffered a stroke. She was pale and weak, and I could find no pulse.

I grabbed the telephone and dialed her doctor. When there was no answer, I tried to remain calm. Anna's color seemed to be returning, and, encouraged by this sign, I began gently patting and rubbing her arm.

In a few moments she opened her eyes and began to apologize for the funny feeling that had come over her. Her voice was thick and weak, but she insisted that she was all right. I helped her to a chair, and she kept apologizing for her unseemly behavior.

At this point the telephone rang. I took the call while Anna sat weakly in her chair. It was her husband's doctor. Russell had taken a turn for the worse about an hour before. According to the doctor, the old man had seemed to be pulling out of it, but then he seemed to relinquish his hold on life. The physician recommended that Anna get to the hospital as soon as possible.

Russell died that night. Although her doctor was unable to find any cause for Anna's sudden seizure, I will always wonder if that strong-willed, possessive husband had not intended to take his beloved wife along with him.

Mara W. received a telepathic call from her husband's hospital bed that drove her to save his life.

"Rick had come down with a bad case of influenza," she said in her account of the experience, "and I was staying at home with our children while he received medical attention in the hospital. I had just started to drift off that night when I clearly heard Rick's voice calling to me: "Honey, I'm dying. Help me! Help me! I'm dying, but no one knows it!"

Mara did not hesitate to act. She saw no need to attempt a rationalization of the voice. She knew that she had not been dreaming, and she knew that she had heard her husband's voice.

It was after midnight when I arrived at the hospital, and, of course, I was coldly informed that visiting hours were over.

I insisted that they examine my husband. Again, in a crisp, antiseptic manner, I was told that a night nurse had just looked in on my husband and that he was sleeping restfully.

I could not be put off. I insisted that they call a doctor to examine him or I would run into that room and look at him myself.

I am not a small woman, and they could see that I meant what I said. They summoned a doctor, who listened wearily to their story and my pleas; then, in order to humor me, he agreed to look in on my husband.

I waited at the desk a few moments, then brushed aside a nurse to run up the stairs that led to my husband's corridor. "Good lord!" I heard the doctor's harsh whisper, "This man is dying!"

Quick work on the part of the doctor and the nurses saved Rick W.'s life.

Later, when he had regained consciousness, Rick told Mara how he had lain there, knowing he was dying, and how he had desperately sought to send a cry for help to her at home. His conviction that his thoughts could make his wife act had saved his life.

CREATE YOUR OWN TELEPATHIC LINK-UP

Experimental psychologist Dr. Stanley Krippner is one of those researchers who feels that the scientific establishment will eventually have to revise its image of humankind on the basis of telepathic evidence. At present, Dr. Krippner observes, psychology and psychiatry view each person as an entity separated from everyone else, as an alienated being.

"Telepathy may teach us that in the basic fabric of life everything and everyone is linked, that man is continuously enmeshed, that he is always an integral part of all life on the face of the earth,"

Dr. Krippner says. "So far the scientific establishment has ignored this possibility; it will, for one thing, refute many of their basic concepts."

Telepathy, as you no doubt understand, simply means that one can, through the mind, make contact with another.

When you experiment with telepathy for the first time, you may find to your surprise that you soon hear from someone whom you have had in mind a great deal, almost as if the person knew you wanted to hear from him.

If you deliberately set out to "reach" someone by your mental telephone, you may encounter a delay in receiving a *physical* response. This should not discourage you, for you will be able to "know" that the telepathic message reached its destination if you felt a mental response at the time.

If you are visualizing the recipient of your message clearly and you suddenly feel a small tingle in your arm or your solar plexus, then you will know that your message has been received on some level of the person's consciousness. You don't have to imagine this response, for it will be real enough.

MAKING TELEPATHIC TRANSFER

It is best to sit quietly for a few moments before attempting a telepathic transfer.

Visualize the vastness of space. Contemplate the meaninglessness of time.

See yourself as a circle that grows and grows until it occupies the Earth, the galaxy. See yourself blending into a oneness with All-That-Is.

Now visualize the one whom you wish to contact. See him plainly. Feel his presence.

In your mind, speak to him as if he were sitting there before you. Do not speak aloud. Speak to him mentally.

Breathe in comfortably deep breaths; this will give added power to the broadcasting station of the psyche.

Mentally relay the message that you wish your friend or loved one to receive from you. Ask him to call you or to get in touch with you.

You may also send healing thoughts to those who are ill. You must understand, of course, that it is not you who heals, but your act of tuning in to the Infinite Mind that does so.

If someone is bereaved, you may send him or her a comforting thought that the Divine Will has been done and that It will soon send solace.

If you are concerned about someone who has a very bad habit that needs correcting, you may send mental pictures to that individual of his hating that habit so much that he, of his own free choice, will give it up.

A Word of Caution When you send healing thoughts to those who are ill, you must visualize that person as being *completely* healed. You must not permit yourself to see him as he is at the present time, miserable in the throes of the illness. You must actually see him in the desired state of health and *know* that it will be so.

When you visualize your loved one who is plagued with the bad habit, he, too, must be seen as triumphant over the annoyance. You must imagine him as having completely forsaken the habit. Only by seeing the bad habit as negated will it be discontinued.

The most vital point in telepathically healing or helping is this: You must actually *see* the desired conditions and *know* that it will be so.

RECEIVING IMPRESSIONS OF YOUR LOVER'S TRUE FEELINGS

If you wish to learn how a loved one or a friend really feels about you, make yourself a receiving set for his or her thoughts.

Sit quietly and breathe slowly in comfortably deep breaths.

Picture in your mind that this particular person is sitting or standing there before you, and ask him or her pointblank: "What do you really think of me?"

If you receive a very warm and gentle impulse or tingle, you will immediately become aware of the fact that the person in question loves you. If you receive a cool impulse, the person in question may dislike you or may be deceitful in his dealings with you.

TELEPATHIC TECHNIQUES FROM OLOF JONSSON

One night I was working some ESP experiments with Olof Jonsson, the psychic who participated with Astronaut Edgar Mitchell in the Moon-to-Earth experiment in telepathic transfer during the Apollo 14 flight in February 1971. Olof is perhaps the most powerful physical sensitive in the world today. Under laboratory conditions he has guessed 100 percent correct in run after run with the Zener ESP testing cards—the cross, the square, the wavyline, the circle, and the star. I have witnessed Olof materialize and dematerialize objects and make tables dance across rooms.

Olof suggested that the beginner try his hand at such elementary exercises as guessing people's birthdays when he seeks to develop his "unknown sensory perception." ("It's not *extra*," Olof insists, "only unknown at the present time.") Try to tune in on what someone might have been doing during the day. Or you can throw dice and try to guess what numbers will come up. You can deal cards at random from a deck, toss them face down, and attempt to guess their value.

According to Olof:

Erase everything from your mind. Forget all about those petty things that are troubling you and relax your mind.

Attain peace and calm.

Achieve harmony.

Do not think!

You must release the irritations in your mind and banish all things that disturb you.

You must tell yourself to become calm and peaceful.

You must command yourself to react to no outside distractions. Once you have achieved the proper conditions, you will feel psychic energy and knowing build up within you.

Do not think! That is the difference between the way your conscious and your unconscious mind work.

You must remain absolutely calm at the time your unconscious is controlling your actions.

It is difficult for me to develop an excitement about guessing Zener cards, but I wanted to mind-link with Olof and work the cards with him.

I created a device for nonthought: I concentrated on an enormous snowbank, an endless expanse of white. After I had retained this image for a few moments, there came a certain "knowing" that told me I could draw a star from the deck. I did so.

"Now a circle," Olof said.

I withdrew a circle. I was finding it easier to blank out my conscious mind. I would blank out, then keep shuffling and shuffling until my mind just seemed to move of its own volition and pick out the card I visualized.

"Isn't it a wonderful feeling when the knowing comes?" Olof asked me.

I readily agreed. "It is a strange feeling, but it is definitely not a *thinking*. You receive an image, say, of the circle; and you go shuffle ... shuffle ... shuffle ... then, pop! There it is."

The mental conditions had to be totally right for the next experiment.

After we had each shuffled the deck thoroughly, Olof asked me to draw five cards at random from the complete deck of ESP cards. When I had blindly selected my five cards, Olof quickly withdrew five cards of his own. Then, with our respective cards held behind our backs, we withdrew one card at a time and matched four out of five!

Imagine the odds against such a rumpling of the laws of chance. Two men had selected two sets of four out of five cards that matched in a random selection, then, without knowledge of those cards, had brought them out from behind their backs in matching sequence, four out of five times!

Olof has another method of developing psychic abilities to share with those who may one day wish to develop telepathic prowess:

Simply fill a glass of water and place it on the table before you. Stare at the water for five minutes or so and erase all thoughts from your mind.

Do not think of a thing. Just look at the water.

Once you feel that you have achieved the proper conditions, practice guessing cards from an ESP deck. The glass of water is merely a physical object on which to focus your attention and to permit the unconscious to rise above your conscious mind.

Once you have learned to blank out your conscious mind by concentrating on the glass of water, you will find it easier to achieve the altered state of consciousness for the exercise of your telepathic abilities.

5

OUT-OF-BODY ROMANCE

Do we possess an astral body that can be projected outside of our physical body to soar unhindered through time and space? Can the soul, the mind, travel independently of the body to faraway places? Can the projected mind appear spirit-like before our friends or relatives and relay messages of great meaning?

Dr. Eugene E. Bernard, professor of psychology at North Carolina State University in Raleigh, stated that his in-progress study of such phenomena had convinced him that one out of every one hundred persons has experienced out-of-body projection. Dr. J. B. Rhine, before his death perhaps the most well-known parapsychologist in the world, is reported to have records of more than 10,000 such cases of out-of-body experience (OBE), which had been submitted to him by people from all over the world.

Dr. Bernard has compared the phenomenon of OBE to" . . . lying on a sofa, getting up and seeing your body still lying on the couch."

Psychical researcher Frederic W. H. Meyers called astral projection, the independent journeying forth of the soul, to be the most extraordinary achievement of the human will.

"What can lie further outside any known capacity than the power to cause a semblance of oneself to appear at a distance?" Meyers once wrote. "What can be more a central action—more manifestly the outcome of whatsoever is deepest and most unitary in man's whole being? Of all vital phenomena, I say, this is the most significant!

"This self-projection is the one definite act which it seems as though a man might perform equally well before and after bodily death."

Dr. Charles Tart, a psychologist and lecturer at the University of California in Sacramento, has noted that accounts of OBE can be found throughout history.

"You can go into Egyptian tombs and see diagrams on the walls of how it's supposed to be done. Greek mystic religions apparently had techniques to induce this experience that were the crux of their initiation ceremonies," Dr. Tart said. "It [OBE] seems to be an altered state of consciousness, which is my principal area of research.

"In the Western world we've rejected these states; we deny they exist when in fact we should be asking such things as, 'Is ESP an evolutionary factor just coming in or just dying out?' And yet in other cultures—all Asia, almost—the altered states of consciousness are acknowledged and used."

Numerous accounts of spontaneous out-of-body experience and carefully conducted experiments in controlled mind projection seem to demonstrate that the human psyche can circumvent the physical limitations of time and space. Although our physical bodies may have to exist in a material world—wherein the confining strictures of mass, energy, space, and time shape our environment—it appears that an ethereal part of ourselves, our essential selves, are fully capable of traveling free of our physical bodies.

A number of leading researchers have declared that certain individuals, when terribly ill, severely injured, or at some time when the lifeforce is threatened, have experienced spontaneous OBE and have separated their minds from their bodies.

While doing research for my own study of astral projection, I interviewed a number of "old pros"—gifted individuals who are able to slip in and out of their bodies almost at will. In many of these cases, I became convinced that there existed a definite correlation between out-of-body experience and human sexual nature. For example, a number of those who reported OBE stated that the experience had taken place during orgasm. And it soon became rather apparent that many deliberate astral projections have been frankly sexual in motivation.

The students of Professor Duncan R. would be astounded, I am certain, to learn that their venerable teacher is in the "old pro" category when it comes to astral projection.

"I cannot normally slip in and out quite as fast as could someone like Oliver Fox or Slyvan Muldoon," he said, "but I have this friend who is a hypnotist and he can zip me out in practically no time at all."

Professor R. admits that one of his most dramatic early projections was sexual in motivation.

I had been going with this delightful creature, who, in today's jargon, would be termed a "swinger." At any rate, she was a flapper who was a real "It" girl, and she was sexually generous without being promiscuous. That may sound like a paradox to some people, but that fellow Hefner in Chicago with his Playboy *philosophy is trying to pass off the same male concept of an ideal bedmate today.*

This girl, we'll call her Lulu, was definitely not the sort one would take home to dear old Mother, and as I was in my wild-oat sowing period at the time, she was just what the medicine man ordered.

It didn't bother me at all to know that I was not the only collegian who shared Lulu's favors. In fact, we had an informal club made up of college men who slept with the townie with the bee-stung lips and the Clara Bow hairdo. "Lulu's Lovers" we called ourselves.

There came this time when Lulu went on a brief vacation and mercilessly left her club members to their own resources. Most of us had regular "nice" girls with whom we could hold hands and maybe even neck with a bit in the back rows of the movie theater, so the deprivation was not really all that bad.

But this one night when my girlfriend had left me all steamed up without cooling me off, I went back to my room and decided to try an experiment. I had long before run across references to astral projection in some old occult books that belonged to my uncle. In addition, I had acquired a few numbers of England's Occult Review *for the year 1920*, which carried some of Oliver Fox's theories and suggestions on attaining controlled out-of-body projection. I had had some quite wonderful experiences, and I had, on numerous occasions, obtained at least subjective proof of my astral travels.

It always took me a while to attain the proper "feel" that enabled me to project my astral body, but I hoped on that particular night my physical need would prod my psyche. I happened to be one of the few fellows who knew where Lulu was staying, and I wrote the address on a slip of paper and began to concentrate on it.

Within a few moments, I had the familiar feeling that my entire conscious self was rolling up in a ball and was moving toward my skull. There was the slight pop, and I was standing outside of my physical body—or rather floating above it—looking down at myself stretched out on the bed.

I thought again of Lulu's address. There came a crackling, electrical sound, and then I seemed to be caught up in a violent wind. The night sky, stars, people, faces, buildings, bright lights—all rushed by me. And then I was there.

My greatest gamble, of course, was that Lulu would be in her room—alone. But as the hour was quite late, and Lulu had told everyone that she was going away on a vacation, "just to be alone, fer gawdsake," I thought that my chances of finding her asleep in bed were quite good.

I was in luck. The sleeping form of Lulu lay stretched out beneath me. How lovely she looked. Lovely and accessible.

I bobbed about the room for a minute or two, noticing certain details about the furniture and the decor. I made a practice of doing this whenever I felt I had achieved astral projection so that I might later substantiate the experience. Then it was back to the business at hand.

I knew from past experience that Lulu slept in the nude, but now she lay beneath me with the bedclothes tucked tightly beneath her chin. Could I simply reach down and lift the covers from her body? I had never tried touching anyone or anything on any of my previous astral travels. Somehow I was afraid even to attempt it. Instead, I tried impressing the thought on Lulu's mind that she should kick off her covers.

After several moments of concentration, I was astonished to see Lulu begin to toss restlessly. An irritated whimper escaped her lips, and, with a great sigh, she flipped the covers from her gloriously naked body.

Now the objective lay directly beneath me. The "spirit" was indeed willing, but what is the spirit in such matters without the flesh?

A movement in a corner of the room startled me. Had I overlooked another presence in the room?

Someone was standing there beside a bed. As I peered into the blackness, I was suddenly struck with the awesome realization that I was seeing my own reflection in a mirror.

This was the first time that I had been able to discern such an image. On previous astral journeys, I had merely been an invisible presence. But now, even though the form was misty and presented only a dim outline, there did seem to be a certain substance to my astral image. Perhaps my desire had added weight to my psyche!

Deciding to waste no more time, I lowered myself between Lulu's outstretched thighs. Could she feel me entering her? As if in answer to my mental question, Lulu's eyes flicked open, widened briefly as they ostensibly beheld my shimmering, spectral image, then closed again. Evidently, if she really had seen me, she had quickly concluded that she was dreaming.

As I began the rhythmic thrusts of love, Lulu moaned, and without opening her eyes, started to rock her hips to match my pace.

Just as I could feel the both of us beginning to come, I seemed suddenly sucked into a black, spiraling vortex. After a few moments, when I opened my eyes, I was back in my physical body on my bed. The first thing that I noticed after a bit more consciousness had returned to me was that my pajama bottoms were soaked with semen. Had I merely had a wet dream, or had I really projected myself to Lulu's vacation apartment?

I was not to know the answer until our girl returned from her hiatus. I made a date with Lulu as soon as I could. After we had had dinner and observed certain social amenities, we lay on her bed smoking cigarettes.

"How was your vacation?" I asked her.

"Just swell, sport," she winked. "When Lulu goes, she goes first class."

At this point she proceeded to describe the "elegant" room in which she had stayed. She made it sound like the Ritz, but I thought I knew better.

When she paused in her lavish description, I interrupted her by saying that that was not at all how I had pictured her room in my imagination. Lulu arched a quizzical, well-plucked eyebrow, and I described the room that I had seen in my projection as well as I could from memory.

Lulu opened her bee-stung lips in a little gasp of surprise. Then her eyes suddenly widened, and she sat up as if a certain unadmitted and unwanted memory was suddenly rushing back to her. "So you were the bastard!" she said. "How in hell did you do it?"

I tried to play it light, but Lulu would have none of it. She ordered me out of her room and refused to ever see me again.

Later I heard that she had told it all over the hangouts that I was a warlock, a male witch. Of course no one believed that, but a lot of the gals and fellows interpreted Lulu's story to mean that I was some kind of sexual deviate who had tried to force her into performing perverted sex practices. I had quite a time of it there for a while, and I have never experimented with out-of-body sex again!

OBE AT THE MOMENT OF ORGASM

A number of men and women have described out-of-body projections at the moment of orgasm during sexual intercourse. As we have previously mentioned, OBE generally occurs when the physical body is fatigued, ill, injured, or when the lifeforce is threatened. It appears that we must not rule out the occurrence of OBE during the ecstasy of sexual orgasm. The sublime pleasure and pain of sexual intercourse is, after all, an active expression of the lifeforce, and it should not surprise us that the making of love (and, possibly, a new life) may be as psychically potent as the threat of death.

Shortly after I had completed work on my first casebook of out-of-body experiences, *The Mind Travelers* (1968), I was told this story by a man who recalled being "cured" of masturbatory practices when he slipped into an OBE.

> *It was about 1949. I was just thirteen and I had been obtaining sexual release via self-gratification for several months. One time this college guy at the YMCA gave us a lecture about how masturbation would lead to loss of strength and virility and how it could even make you have a nervous breakdown or go nuts if you did it often enough. You know, it was one of those old-fashioned "scare hell out of 'em, but don't bother to really explain anything" types of talks.*
>
> *I figured the guy was just a holy joe giving us a line. He was about twenty-two, and we knew he was studying for the ministry. So I figured, you know, he just had to say things like that as part of his practicing for the pulpit.*
>
> *Any way, that night I went to see this sexy movie without my folks knowing it. By today's standards, of course, it was like the Bobbsey Twins nuzzling noses with Rebecca of Sunnybrook Farm. But everything is relative, you know, and it boiled my brains and my tender young testes.*
>
> *I went to my room as soon as I got home and headed right for the covers and lights out. I was fantasizing like hell and rubbing my penis for all it was worth. Then I came and* went

at the same time. I mean, it must have been the potency of that adolescent orgasm that just shot me right out of the body.

I could feel myself floating up to the ceiling, like I was a crazy balloon on a string. Then I could look down and see myself lying still on the bed. I mean, I could see my backside. I had always wondered what I looked like from the back, and now I was able to see.

"Jeez, I thought, not only did I go insane—I died!

Then my body on the bed below gave a long sigh, took a deep breath, and I was back inside my body. I didn't masturbate again for years!

BETWEEN WAKING AND SLEEPING

A high percentage of the experiences reported in this book have occurred during the hypnagogic state of consciousness that lies between waking and sleeping. It seems that when the conscious mind has relinquished most, but not quite all, of its control over the personality, the unconscious is able to reach out to "tune in" to the true totality of the cosmos.

A similar altered state of consciousness exists during hypnotic trance, which may indicate that out-of-body experience may be controlled by certain talented people in somewhat the same manner that telepathy, clairvoyance, and precognition seem to be mentally domesticated by men and women whom we call "psychic sensitives."

One evening Gordon North had worked late. It was nearly ten o'clock before he returned home. There were few lights left on in his house, but as he opened the door, he thought he caught a glimpse of Karen, his wife of three months, hiding in a corner of the front room.

Believing the playful Karen sought to tease him, Gordon pretended not to see her, then suddenly whirled toward the spot where she crouched behind a piece of furniture. Karen managed to evade him, and she danced lightly out of the reach of his arms. Gordon pursued his wife about the room, but she moved always just out of his grasp.

At last Gordon darted forward and laughingly cornered his wife by the wall. He gave a shout of triumph, but as he was about to throw his arms around her he heard a peculiar sound—like a report of a faraway rifle—and Karen vanished before his astonished eyes.

He stepped back from the wall, his brain literally throbbing in an effort to classify the incident he had just witnessed.

"Gordon, what on earth are you doing out in the living room?" It was Karen's voice coming from the bedroom. "What is all that noise?"

Gordon North found his wife curled up in bed, where she insisted she had been all the time, having grown weary of waiting up for him.

Trudy C. saw her husband's double one night as he lay sleeping beside her. She recalls:

I was sleeping very restlessly that night. We had gone to bed too early, really, and now it was only a little past midnight and I had awakened.

As I turned my head toward my husband, I saw a most remarkable thing. Jim's astral body, or soul, was rising out of his physical body. It sat up beside him for a moment; then it got up and walked toward the bathroom door.

I knew that I was wide awake, and I was just a little frightened. "Where are you going, Jim?" I called after the astral Jim, but, of course, it paid no attention to me. The physical Jim still lay sleeping peacefully beside me. The astral body of my husband stood before the bathroom door, as if undecided whether or not it should leave the bedroom.

I was able to get a good look at Jim's astral body as it walked across the room. It was identical to Jim's physical body—red hair, same pajamas, everything. His astral body, though, had a silver glow around it, and it was transparent. I could see Jim's soul distinctly, and yet I could see through it.

Trudy closed her eyes for a few moments and prayed that all was well with her husband. When she opened her eyes again, Jim's soul body had returned to his physical shell, and her husband lay sleeping restfully beside her.

The experience convinced Trudy C. that it is possible for the soul to exist outside the body while the physical body lies in sleep or in trance. She also believes that the incident provided her with proof that the soul goes on living after the death of the physical body.

Ernest Mundo has written about his near-death experience:

> *I thought I was dead that night when that automobile struck mine at the intersection. What seemed to be the* real *me was somewhere above the wreck looking down at all the confusion. I saw the police and the crowd arrive, and I could see my bleeding body slumped forward on the steering wheel. This is it, I thought, I'm dead.*
>
> *I wanted to see Laura one last time. I had only to form the thought and I was there, watching her fix dinner, completely unaware of either the accident or my soul there behind her.*
>
> *I thought of our only son, who lived in Phoenix. In an instant I was bobbing above him as he sat at his desk in an office.*
>
> *I felt no sorrow at leaving them, but I was thankful I had been given the opportunity to see them one last time.*
>
> *Then I seemed to feel a tugging and a pulling, and I was being sucked back in a brilliant, swirling blur of color and light.*
>
> *I landed in my body with a jerk, and I heard a voice say, "Jeez, doc, what's in that needle? It really snapped him back to life." I heard another man chuckle, and I opened my eyes to see what appeared to be dozens of people pressing forward. I caught a glimpse of the back of a police officer herding the curiosity-seekers away from my automobile; then a sickening rush of pain caused me to lapse back into unconsciousness.*
>
> *This time there was no journey, and I awakened several hours later in a hospital bed with my wife holding my hand.*

CONTROLLING
OUT-OF-BODY PROJECTION

In the attainment of ESP abilities, I believe very strongly that the "gifts" of prophecy, clairvoyance, telepathy, psychometry, and so forth, will be developed much sooner if one uses altered states of consciousness (ASC). I also believe that the ability to control OBE is extremely important as a tool in the fashioning of more complete talents of the psyche. Astral travel opens the doorways to all other facets of spirit. Once you have learned to project your spirit from its temple of flesh, all other paranormal talents will be added unto you.

I am now going to present a color meditation that can place you into a deep altered state within which you can use the Love Force to accomplish astral travel. Be optimistic and positive. By the same token, expect that it may take you more than one session to become an expert mind traveler.

Since this technique deals with color and with repetitious progressions, it is quite easy to memorize and to place yourself in an altered state. Or you may wish to record a cassette of your voice ahead of time and thereby become your own guide through the experience. If you have a like-minded friend or family member to guide you, so much the better.

You will find it extremely helpful to play a recording of the proper music to suggest a mood of "lifting" away. Any music that you find swelling or inspiring will do. Just be certain that it is instrumental only, for lyrics will distract you by suggesting images other than the ones desired. I, personally, recommend Steven Halpern's *Starborn Suite* for meditation and for achieving altered states.

Sit in a chair, lie on your bed, lean against a wall—whatever position is most comfortable for you. Select a time when you will not be disturbed. Disconnect the telephone. Turn on your music.

Visualize that at your feet lies a blanket the color of rose. The color of rose stimulates natural body warmth and induces sleep. It also provides one with a sense of well-being and a great feeling of being loved.

Now you see that the blanket is really a kind of auric cover, a rose-colored auric cover. Imagine that you are willing the blanketlike aura of rose to move slowly up your body.

Feel it moving over your feet, relaxing them; over your legs, relaxing them; over your stomach, easing all tensions; moving over your chest, your arms, your neck.

Now, as you make a hood of the rose-colored auric cover, imagine that the color of rose permeates your psyche and does its part in activating your ability to become one with the Love Force. Once you have done this, visualize yourself bringing the rose-colored aura over your head.

The color green serves as a disinfectant, a cleanser. It also influences the proper building of muscles and tissue.

Imagine that you are pulling a green, blanketlike aura over your body. Feel it moving over your feet, cleansing them; feel it moving over your legs, healing them of all pains. Feel it moving over your stomach, ridding it of all pains. Feel it moving over your chest, your arms, your neck—cleansing them, healing them.

As you make a hood of the green-colored auric cover, imagine that the color of green permeates your psyche and does its part in activating your ability to use the Love Force for healing. Once you have done this, visualize yourself bringing the green-colored aura over your head.

Gold has been recognized as a great strengthener of the nervous system. It also aids digestion and helps you to become calm.

Visualize now that you are pulling a soft, beautiful golden aura slowly over your body. Feel it moving over your feet, calming you. Feel it moving over your legs, relaxing them. Feel it moving over your stomach, soothing any nervous condition. Feel it moving over your chest, your arms, your neck.

As you make a comfortable hood of the golden aura, imagine that the color of gold permeates your psyche and strengthens your nervous system so that your body-brain network will serve as a better conduit for the Love Force. Once you have done this, visualize yourself bringing the gold-colored aura over your head.

Researchers have discovered that red-orange strengthens and cleanses the lungs. Yogis and other masters have long known that effective meditation, effective ASC, can best be achieved through proper techniques of breathing through clean lungs.

Visualize before you a red-orange color of pure oxygen. Take a comfortably deep breath and visualize some of that red-orange cloud moving into your lungs. Imagine it traveling through your lungs, cleansing them, purifying them, taking away particles of impurities.

Now visualize yourself *exhaling* that red-orange cloud of oxygen from your lungs. See how soiled with impurities it is.

Take another comfortably deep breath. See again the red-orange cloud of pure, clean oxygen moving into your lungs. See the red-orange cloud purifying your lungs of the negative effects of exhaust fumes, smoke, and other pollution. Exhale the impurities, then breathe again of the purifying, cleansing red-orange cloud.

Yellow-orange aids oxygen in moving into every organ and gland of your body, purifying them, cleansing them.

Imagine before you now a yellow-orange cloud of pure oxygen. Take a comfortably deep breath and inhale that cleansing, purifying yellow-orange cloud into your lungs. Feel the yellow-orange cloud moving through your body. Feel it cleansing and purifying every organ. Feel it cleansing and purifying every gland. If you have *any* area of weakness or disease *anywhere* in your body, feel the yellow-orange energy bathing it in cleansing, healing vibrations.

As you exhale all impurities and inhale again the pure yellow-orange cloud of oxygen, visualize the cleansing and healing process throughout your body. As you exhale and inhale, see your body becoming pure and clean.

Blue is the color of psychic ability, the color that increases visionary potential.

Visualize a blue blanketlike aura beginning to move over your body. Feel it moving over your feet, relaxing them. Feel it moving over your legs, soothing them. Feel it moving over your stomach, your chest, your arms, your neck—soothing them, relaxing them.

As you make a hood of the blue-colored auric cover, imagine that the color of blue permeates your psyche and does its part in activating your ability to use the Love Force for telepathy, clairvoyance, psychokinesis, and prophecy. Once you have done this, visualize yourself bringing the blue-colored aura over your head.

Violet is the color of the highest vibration.

Imagine that you are pulling a violet, blanketlike aura over your body. Feel it moving over your feet, relaxing them. Feel it moving over your legs, relaxing them, soothing them. Feel it moving over your stomach, removing all tensions. Feel it moving over your chest, your arms, your neck—tranquilizing them, relaxing them.

Now, as you fashion a hood of the violet-colored auric cover, imagine that the color of violet permeates your psyche and does its part in activating your ability to use the Love Force. Feel the color violet attuning your psyche to the highest vibration. Feel the color violet connecting your psyche to the Source of All-That-Is. Once you have done this, visualize yourself bringing the violet-colored aura over your head.

You are now lying or sitting totally wrapped in your violet-colored auric cover. You are very secure, very comfortable, very relaxed. Your mind is very receptive, very aware. You feel attuned with the Love Force. You feel as though your awareness has been expanded. You feel prepared to explore deep, deep within you, deep, deep within you.

[For the next portion of this exercise, I recommend *Tarashanti* by Georgia Kelley, or any record of restful flute music.]

You are seeing memory patterns before you. They may be your memories of a past life experience. They may be the memories of another. It does not matter. You are seeing them taking form before you now.

The energy of the Love Force is taking you to a faraway place, a faraway time on the vibrations of the Eternal Now. You are seeing blue, blue sky. Ocean. Mountains. A large temple made of stone high in the mountains. You are remembering an ancient temple hidden in time.

You are remembering that you were a student there, a very special student of a very special teacher—a priest or priestess who taught unconditional love and the oneness of the Love Force.

This great teacher has made you a prize pupil. You, more than any of the other initiates, have responded perfectly to the sound of the wondrous flute of universal love. When the teacher blows the flute, you are able to leave your body. When you hear the flute, you soar free of your physical limitations. You soar high above the mountains. You soar free of time and space. You can go anywhere you wish—instantly. You have but to think it, and you will be there.

You are proud that you have become your master's special student. You are proud that of all the students in this great city of love, you are the one who has been selected for the great demonstration.

Now you are walking through the corridors of the temple, surrounded by the other students.

You are walking to a special room in the temple where you will give the demonstration.

Look around you. Remember the faces of those nearest you. Remember the pillars of the temple, the tapestry, the candles, the statues.

Now you are approaching the place of the demonstration. It is a beautiful room, draped in violet. You see that your master-teacher is already there. He or she holds a magic flute.

Twelve students step forward from the crowd and form a circle around an altar.

You step into the circle, advance to the altar. You take a deep breath and lie down on a violet blanket.

You look up at the curved ceiling of the chamber. A small cloud of incense floats toward its arch. You lie quietly for a few moments, then raise an arm to signal that you are ready.

You lie there on the blanket, on your back, looking up at the curved ceiling. You are calm. You are relaxed. You know that when you hear the sound of the flute of love, you will soar free of your body. Your essential self, the Real You that exists within, will burst free of the limitations of the physical body and shoot up through the ceiling toward the moon, toward someone whom you love.

Your teacher lifts the flute and blows.

You feel yourself rushing, pushing, pulsating, spinning—bursting free of the body!

You, the *real you*, soars through the temple ceiling toward the moon.

Down below you can see the students, your teacher. But your universe is only you and the sound, the sound of the magic flute of love.

Go with the sound. Go to whomever you wish. You have but to think of the person, and you will be with him or her instantly.

Think of a loved one who is far away. You have but to think of that loved one and you will be there instantly. You will be beside that loved one *instantly*.

The sound takes you there. The sound takes you to be at the side of your loved one. Go with the sound! Go with the Love Force!

Practice this technique every other night for as long as it takes for you to accomplish a successful projection. You may continue to use the color meditation to place yourself into a deep altered state.

Once you have successfully traveled to a few target areas and successfully viewed faraway loved ones, your own creative principle will begin to suggest variations on the exercise.

Whether an OBE is but an imaginative manner in which to express telepathy or traveling clairvoyance is a question that some parapsychologists enjoy arguing. Such a matter need not concern those of us who travel in the energy of the Love Force. We are pragmatists. We are primarily interested in the results we attain.

The instructions and exercises shared thoughout this book may be practiced with several variations, and the able student will invent numerous applications of his or her own for each example.

The mastery of psi abilities is important for your general growth in the Love Force. The manifestation of disciplined out-of-body projections, clairvoyance, telepathy, and so forth, are all necessary ingredients in the cosmic crucible that transforms flesh to spirit.

6

LOVERS WHO TRANSCENDED

Silvia Waddell had not really expected to sleep well on that August night in 1968. Her husband Stanley lay in a coma in General Hospital, and his doctor had informed her that the end was near.

"There's nothing more that you can do here," the physician had advised her. "Why don't you leave the hospital and get some rest?"

Silvia had explained to the doctor that she felt that her place must be at her husband's bedside.

"What if he should awaken and not find me there?" she had asked. "And it is too far to drive home only to come back if he needs me."

"Your husband has not been conscious for days," the doctor had said. "You appear to be on the brink of exhaustion. What good can you be to your children if you end up sick and in the hospital yourself? Get a room in a hotel near the hospital. Let the front desk know your number as soon as you've registered. I promise to call you if there is any change in your husband's condition."

Silvia had caught a glimpse of herself in a large corridor window that the night's blackness had turned into a mirror. Her red-rimmed eyes looked deep-set because of the dark circles beneath them. Her hair was unkempt, disarrayed. Her face was puffy from crying, wan from lack of sleep. Perhaps the doctor was right, she had decided. She had better get some rest.

Now she lay beneath crisp hotel sheets, hoping that the drone of the air conditioner might lull her to sleep. She checked her watch for what must have been the twentieth time since she had lain down shortly after midnight. It was 3:47 A.M.

Then, strangely, Silvia sensed a familiar presence.

"Stan," she whispered, as she turned over on her back and sat up in bed.

She could see her husband clearly in the dim light of the hotel room. Somehow, in a manner that she would never be able to understand, Stanley stood at her bedside.

"I am leaving you now," Stanley said. His voice was full and rich, as it had been before the terrible illness had wasted his strength, his body, even the timbre of his speech. "This old shell I've been using is no longer of any value to me. Don't worry. I'll always watch over you and our baby daughter."

Silvia sat motionless long after the image of her husband had faded from the room. She was convinced that Stan was dead, that his spirit had actually come to bid her good-bye, but grief had not been able to penetrate the dazed mental condition in which the sudden appearance of the apparition had left her. The part of her brain that was still thinking, still functioning, kept expecting the hospital to call and inform her of Stanley's death.

The call did not come until 10:00 A.M., more than six hours after her husband's apparition had appeared to her.

After she had attended to some of the details at the hospital, Silvia asked to see her husband's ward doctor. When the physician asked politely if there were something that he might do for her, she asked if she could see her husband's chart.

"That's highly irregular and against hospital rules," the doctor began, then, struck by something in Silvia's manner, he ceased his mechanical recitation of hospital dogma. "Why do you wish to see your husband's chart, Mrs. Waddell?"

"I would very much like to verify the precise moment of my husband's death," she explained. "I . . . I have a strong conviction that Stanley died at 3:47 A.M., even though the hospital did not phone me until 10:00 A.M. Please, doctor," she said softly, "it is very important to me to know this."

The physician called to a nurse seated at a desk to bring Stanley Waddell's chart. When he had it in his hand his eyebrows raised. He showed the chart to Silvia, his forefinger pointing to the time of death—3:47 A.M.

Her eyes brimmed with tears. She had not been dreaming. Stan had appeared to her. Her beloved husband had come to bid her good-bye and to offer her dramatic evidence of the human personality's ability to survive the death experience.

As she turned to leave the ward, the nurse touched Silvia gently on the arm. "You knew, didn't you? Somehow you knew the exact moment your husband's soul left his body."

Silvia nodded, unable to speak in her deep emotion.

"Someday," the nurse said, "I pray that I might experience proof of the soul's survival after death."

This chapter discusses accounts of men and women whose dying loved ones seemed to have given them dramatic evidence of the soul's continued existence after the physical death of the body. Documented stories of such apparitions may be found in the literature of all eras and all cultures. Images of loved ones who have come to say farewell—to offer comfort and solace before their transition to another plane or existence—appear to rich and to poor alike.

The doubts of the skeptical have no relevancy to those men and women who have witnessed the apparition of a dear mate or sweetheart at the moment of their death or to those researchers who have spent many years of serious inquiry into the matter. As Andrew Lang once wrote: "Only one thing is certain about apparitions, namely, they do appear. They are really perceived."

The remaining question is whether the percipients actually observed a discarnate entity, which occupied an objective area in time and space, or whether they perceived the result of a successfully implanted telepathic message-image, which had been transmitted at the moment of death by the dying loved one.

Whether the percipients about whom you are going to read were truly visited by the discarnate personalities of their loved ones, or whether they received a last telepathic message that became externalized by their own minds, we cannot dismiss their experiences as simply dramatic devices of their imaginations. In each of the cases the apparitions left the percipient with some bit of veridical information, information that was previously unknown to the percipient and that could be later verified (e.g., Silvia Waddell learning that the apparition of her husband appeared to her at the actual time of his death).

This would seem to be the place to distinguish the various differences between the disparate phenomena known as apparitions and ghosts.

A ghost appears at the same place at regular intervals, like a bit of motion-picture film that keeps being replayed whenever someone of the proper telepathic affinity sets the psychic "projector" into operation. A ghost seldom conveys any information to the percipient; indeed, a ghost rarely notices or interacts with a percipient in any way. Perhaps a ghost may best be defined as an animated memory pattern somehow attached to a place where a scene of strong emotion may have occurred.

An apparition, on the other hand, is always known and identified by the percipient. An apparition seldom appears more than once, and nearly always delivers information that is immediately intelligible and personally meaningful to the percipient.

Whether such apparitions represent a last cry of love from the innermost spirit or an *au revoir* to a loved from the actual discarnate spirit, the following accounts gave inestimable solace to the surviving lovers.

An account reached me not long ago of how a man received what was to him convincing subjective proof that the human personality survives the death experience.

Charles Flandre had left the bedside of his wife, Laura, who was dying of leukemia. The ordeal had been a long and painful one for his poor wife, as well as being expensive and exhausting for Charles.

"Please go home and get some rest," Laura said. "You must not stay here another night worrying over me. Go home and see to the children."

Flandre told his wife that he would go home, look in on the children and her mother, who had come to help with baby-sitting and the housework, but that he would come back to the hospital to be at her side. Laura only smiled. Flandre recalled:

I saw that the children were all right and that Laura's mother had already gone to bed, Flandre recalled. I checked my watch, then I decided to nap for just a few minutes before I returned to the hospital.

I couldn't have been sleeping more than twenty minutes when I felt what I knew to be the touch of my wife's lips on my cheek. It was a kiss of sweetness and love, a kiss that only Laura could have given me. No one will ever be able to convince me that it was not my wife who kissed me at that moment.

I opened my eyes and sat up. I had left a small lamp on in the room before I had lain down to rest. I knew that someone else was in that room.

Then, in a darkened corner, I caught a movement out of the corner of my eye. I turned to see a figure that seemed to be formed from a million tiny, sparkling stars. Although I could distinguish no features, the figure had a human-like shape. It seemed to raise its arms and float up out of sight through the ceiling.

When I called the hospital a few moments later, I was not surprised to learn that Laura had just died. The night nurse had just been about to call me. She spoke a few words to console me, but I had just received the greatest kind of consolation from my Laura, who had come to prove to me that there is life beyond physical death.

Although Norma Stentor knew that her father William Harbot had hardening of the arteries and often became mentally confused, she became very annoyed by the fact that he had referred to her mother as "that old lady" when she had died in September 1973.

The Harbots had been for a walk in the small park above their home when Esther Harbot suffered a sudden stroke and fell to the sidewalk. Harbot had been leaning on his cane with one hand and resting his arm on his wife when she made a gasping sound and collapsed.

Harbot was carried to the ground by the force of her fall, and the two elderly people had been found pitifully intertwined. Esther Harbot died without regaining consciousness, and Mr. Harbot was brought to the residence of his daughter, Norma Stentor, seemingly more confused than ever.

"Esther was dying and leaving me," he told her. "I wanted to talk with her longer, but that old lady knocked into me and we both fell to the sidewalk. How I wish that she hadn't knocked me down."

Norma wrote:

I had been so shattered by the loss of my mother that it was difficult to be patient with Dad. He seemed to be concerned only that Mother had knocked him down when she died. And it offended me that he kept referring to her as "that old lady."

Norma resolved to be as compassionate as possible, and for several months she simply "tuned out" whatever her father had to say about her mother's death.

Then one day he said something that made her listen to his mumblings with interest. "I wonder," Harbot mused into space, "if that old lady died, too."

"What do you mean when you wonder if *she* died, *too*?" Norma asked. "Tell me again how Mother died."

Harbot began

We were walking in the park, like we always loved to do. Then Esther stopped me, and said that she was sorry, but that it was time for her to go—to die. I begged her not to leave me, but she left my side and began to walk down the hill toward the pond where the swans swim. A golden shaft of light came down from the sky, and two tall men in flowing robes stepped forward to take Esther by the hand. I called to her again, and she turned as if to tell me good-bye. But I never heard what she said, because that was when that old lady stumbled against me and knocked me down.

In her account of the experience, Norma Stentor wrote that for the first time she realized that her father had not associated Esther, her mother, with the "old lady" who had pulled him down with her to the sidewalk.

Upon further questioning, Norma learned that, in his mental confusion, her father had seen his wife as she had appeared when she was much younger. The apparition that had come to tell him farewell was an image of his Esther in the full bloom of her womanhood, not the wrinkled "old lady" who had knocked him down at such an inopportune moment.

The case of William Harbot seems to argue for the theory that that the apparition is the result of a successfully implanted telepathic message that becomes externalized by the percipient's own mind. The confused mental processes of the elderly Mr. Harbot perceived his Esther as she once was, not as she existed at the moment of her death. If the apparition were truly a discarnate entity occupying an objective bit of time and space, then Mrs. Harbot should have said good-bye as the elderly woman she really was.

We must be careful not to become dogmatic in an area about which we know so little, however. Perhaps these images that come to say farewell to loved ones and to impart a bit of veridical information may be just what they seem to be—truth-telling, leave-taking spirits of the beloved. Perhaps the mental machinery of William Harbot, who suffered from hardening of the arteries, would have perceived his wife as a younger woman even if her discarnate soul had appeared to him in the form of the elderly woman she was at the moment of her death. How many of us have witnessed elderly grandparents addressing our parents as if they were still children, rather than the middle-aged men and women who stand there in the reality of the present moment?

ARE WE REUNITED IN THE SPIRIT WORLD?

One of the great questions that men and women ask is whether or not lovers are reunited in the spirit world after death. Then, almost in the same breath, they wonder if a lover who has passed on maintains his love for the surviving partner. And what if the survivor of the marriage or love affair finds another earthly lover? Does the deceased lover become jealous, or does he now exist beyond petty concerns of the flesh?

Alson J. Smith, author of *Immortality, the Scientific Evidence*, once spoke on the question of marriage in the spirit world and said that he did not believe that two souls would be reunited as husband and wife.

"I think they recognize and love each other," Smith said, "but marriage is an earthly institution with a physical basis; there is no need for such an institution or basis in the spirit world."

It was Smith's personal belief that *husband* and *wife* were meaningless terms in the spirit world; on such a plane of existence there would be only individuals who had achieved higher levels of understanding and deeper insights than they had known on earth.

"The widow who remarries will be joined not only by her two earthly husbands, but by all who have achieved her level of understanding. It is only our physicalistic, limited thinking that makes this idea unattractive to us."

Lois Barker writes that she attended Communion the day after her husband had been laid to rest. "I had attended the early service that Sunday, and my thoughts were filled with anguish as I contemplated the long years ahead without my husband."

Lois said that she then sensed a presence next to her in the pew, kneeling beside her.

"I knew that it was my husband, but I did not turn to look. I did not want to do anything to destroy the impression I had of his presence. I wanted to hold on to the feeling that John had actually returned to take Communion with me."

When Lois Barker went forward to receive the sacraments at the altar rail, she felt that the presence of her husband walked with her. But after she had knelt to receive the wafer and the wine, she sensed that John had once again left her.

A few days, later, when she was visiting with her priest, the clergyman told her that he had had a most unusual experience at the early Communion service on Sunday.

"As I was turning to face the altar," he said, "I had the most peculiar feeling that your husband had come in and knelt down beside you. When you walked to the altar to receive the sacraments, I had to blink my eyes. It almost seemed as though I could perceive a dim outline of John standing just behind you."

Again, whether the spirit of a dead husband or the manifestation of a telepathic impulse caused both the widow and her priest to sense the presence of the deceased is a moot point. Whatever the explanation, Lois Barker received spiritual comfort from the belief that her husband's spirit had joined her in church that Sunday morning to partake of a farewell Communion service with her.

INHABITANTS OF THE INVISIBLE WORLD

John Frederick Oberlin, the famous pastor, educator, and philanthropist, had his universe expanded when he was assigned to the Ban-de-la-Roche valley in the Vosges Mountains of Alsace. Shortly after the clergyman's arrival in the district, he expressed his immediate and earnest displeasure regarding the superstitions of the natives. Pastor Oberlin became especially agitated over the villagers' reports about the apparitions of dying loved ones. The new pastor resolved to educate the simple folk, and he launched a vociferous pulpit campaign against such superstitious tales.

In spite of his orthodox denial of apparitions, the reports of such phenomena continued unabated, and Pastor Oberlin was honest enough to admit that he was beginning to feel his dogma crumbling around him.

In 1806 a dreadful avalanche at Rossberg buried several villages, and the reports of visions of the dying appearing to loved ones became so numerous that Pastor Oberlin at last came to believe that the villagers were indeed perceiving spirits of the departed.

In *Footfalls on the Boundary of Another World*, Robert Dale Owen tells us that Oberlin came to believe that his own wife appeared to him after her death. The clergyman maintained that his wife's spirit watched over him as though she were a guardian angel. Furthermore, Pastor Oberlin claimed that he could see his wife's spirit, talk with her, and make use of her counsel regarding future events.

When a skeptic asked the cleric how he was certain that he could distinguish his wife's spirit communications from the fantasy of dreams, Oberlin replied: "How do you distinguish one color from another?"

Oberlin compiled extensive manuscripts describing in detail a series of manifestations in which his wife appeared to him and dictated information regarding life after death. Owen quotes a Frenchman named Matter who visited Pastor Oberlin to discuss his beliefs with him: "Oberlin was convinced that the inhabitants of the invisible world can appear to us, and we to them, when God wills; and that we are apparitions to them, as they to us."

A young woman who visited some friends in Milwaukee, Wisconsin, found out just how real those inhabitants of the invisible world can seem. Kathy Mueller wrote:

> Marilyn Erickson and I had roomed together for two semesters. When she invited me to her home to spend the weekend, I was looking forward to a fun time in Beer City. As it turned out, the Ericksons were teetotalers and were not interested in the brews that had made Milwaukee famous. I knew that Marilyn drank on campus, but obviously she observed her parents' prejudices when she was at home.
>
> Marilyn and I went to a movie, then came home and watched a late show on television before we went to bed. Maybe I wasn't going to live it up the way I had hoped, but at least I was going to get my rest. I had a nice big bed in an attractive guest room, so, I asked myself, who was I to complain?
>
> Sometime during the night, I was awakened by voices coming from downstairs. They were strained voices, like people having a heated discussion yet trying to hold their voices down.
>
> I have never been able to be as cool and aloof as the modern girl is supposed to be. I am, admittedly, a curious person. I got out of bed, walked partway down the stairs, and leaned over the banister so that I might see who was going at it in the living room.
>
> The house was dark, illumined only by a night light in the upstairs bathroom, yet I could clearly see the figures of a young man and a young woman seated on the large, flowered couch. At first I thought that the young woman was Marilyn, but on second look I could see that the two women only resembled one another, like sisters. Even though the two figures were clearly discernible, there seemed to be a weird kind of fog surrounding them, a billowing mist.

I heard things like, "But you know we mustn't," and "Dad would kill me if he found out," and "You know we must wait." It seemed to me that the age-old agrument of the sexes was going on in the living room between Marilyn's older sister, who for some reason neither she nor her parents had ever mentioned, and an eager boyfriend. I am curious, but I am no voyeur. I decided to return to my bed.

The next morning I asked Marilyn why she never told me that she had a sister. Marilyn paled and asked me what I meant. "Oh, come on," I teased. "She can't be that much of a black sheep. Where is she now? Is she still sleeping in her room? I'd like to meet her."

We were on our way down the stairs to breakfast, but Marilyn caught me by the arm and led me back upstairs to the guest room. "We mustn't let Dad hear this," she whispered.

I could not comprehend why there was such mystery about the errant sister, until we were alone in the guest room.

Marilyn told me that her older sister, Rachael, had eloped with a young man late one night more than seven years before. The two young lovers had been killed in a head-on automobile crash as they drove to Minnesota to be married. Marilyn had been only twelve years old at the time, but she could remember the terrible months of self-recrimination during which her parents had tormented themselves. They had been so strict with Rachael and so disapproving of her boyfriend that they held themselves responsible for the young couple's decision to run away to get married. Since that terrible night, the voices of the two lovers had often been heard in the downstairs living room, where they had so often, during their troubled courtship, discussed their present problems and their hopes for the future.

At first I could not believe what Marilyn was telling me, but I searched all the rooms and could find no evidence that Rachael or any young woman other than Marilyn lived in the Erickson home.

When I persisted in accusing my friend of putting me on, she got out an old scrapbook and showed me pictures of the two girls when they were younger. A photograph of Rachael in a formal *gown, smiling and ready for a prom, really grabbed me. I was certain that she was the girl I had seen in the parlor the night before.*

I guess Marilyn must have told her parents that I had seen the ghosts, or maybe they had lived with the troubled voices long enough, for I learned later that the Ericksons left their home in Milwaukee and moved to another city.

COMMUNICATING WITH THE SPIRIT WORLD

My wife Frances has communicated with the spirit world ever since she was a small child. The only problem she has is that she finds it difficult to distinguish between the physically living and the physically dead. To her, an entity is an entity.

Sometimes we play a little game in which I give her the name of an individual. She describes that person perfectly, often down to the smallest detail.

Then I ask her if that person is alive or dead.

Very often she has to go rather deep within to tell me that answer. Her stream of consciousness that was flowing so quickly begins to dam up a bit until she can attune herself to the present physical state of the entity.

Although some of us—for whatever reason—seem to have innate mediumship abilities, I am convinced that everyone is more or less able to cultivate such talents.

Patience and practice One cannot be dogmatic about which procedures work best for the encouragement of mediumship, but I can say with great certainty that the prime prerequisites are patience and practice.

All psychic development, if it is to be effective and lasting, must grow through a slow and gradual process. Do not attempt to rush your contact, and do not become discouraged if you do not become an overnight success as a medium.

Consider your development as a communicator between worlds as a very serious undertaking.

One of the primary essences of Indian medicine power is a strong belief in the partnership between the world of the physical and the world of the spiritual. If you begin your sitting out of a sense of levity, you are indicating your desire to fail at a most vital and serious project.

Some of you will probably achieve amazing results in a relatively short time. For others, the development of your abilities may take weeks or months.

A regular time As much as possible, set a regular time for your development exercises. Don't overdo this by becoming a slave to the clock or by sitting too often.

Begin with a ten- or-fifteen-minute session every other day, or twice a week. Daily sessions are all right, too.

Gradually increase your time allotment to half an hour a sitting. Don't go beyond that unless and until you reach the stage where manifestations occur regularly and may occasionally require longer periods.

The time of day most suitable for your early exercises and, for that matter, perhaps for all psychic training and experimentation, is the latter part of the evening—when you are finished with the day's responsibilities, when your segment of the world has slowed down to a more serene pace.

The seance room The room in which you sit should be quiet, not too large, and sufficiently remote to assure privacy and safety from interruptions.

The lighting should be subdued. One bulb in a wall socket or a desk lamp is more than adequate—and even that should be shaded, possibly with a blue or a violet scarf or some gauze of similar color.

Complete darkness is, of course, very desirable as well; but sitting alone late at night in total darkness, attempting to make spirit contact, is often a bit unnerving for the novice medium. Let no one tell you that absolute darkness is essential to spirit manifestations.

The expectancy method If you are conducting your experimentations alone—which is not the most desirable arrangement exept for the first part of your training—place yourself in a comfortable chair and use the method that some mediums call "expectancy."

Sit quietly.

Divest your thoughts of your immediate worldly concerns and attempt to keep your mind blank.

Place yourself in as receptive a mood as possible. Be alert, but don't expect anything particular to occur. Be patient and wait.

If you seem to see points of light darting about the room, understand that they could be caused by natural manifestations or eye strain.

If you hear the creaking of floor boards, recognize that the sound may be caused by changes in temperature rather than the appearance of an unseen guest.

If your arms and legs become numb and cold, know that these sensations may be due to tiredness or rigidity, rather than the approach of the supernormal.

In other words, remain calm and don't become panicky or credulous. You will know well enough when the real thing comes.

Adjourn your expectancy sitting after ten or fifteen minutes. Repeat it a day later—or two or three days later—up to a total of a dozen times or more.

If genuine phenomena or raps do occur, don't be surprised and don't be frightened. Such things merely indicate that you are well on the way to mediumship and that you are gaining in psychic strength.

Automatic writing Automatic writing is a method of communicating with the beyond that many men and women find preferable and more adaptable to their personal cosmologies or philosophies.

Seat yourself comfortably at a table.

Place a piece of paper before you and hold a pen or a pencil in your hand in the manner in which you usually write. Let its tip rest lightly on the paper.

Keep your wrist and arm loose, the wrist perferably in such a position that it does not touch the table at all.

Wait quietly and patiently. Close your eyes. Listen to flowing New Age music, such as Steven Halpern's *Starborn Suite*.

Give in to the slightest impulse to move the pencil, keeping the paper smooth with your free hand.

It is not necessary—and in fact not even desirable—that you concentrate on your hand and what it is doing. If you do not wish to keep your eyes closed, you may even read a book while experimenting, just to keep your thoughts occupied.

See to it that no direct light shines on the paper. Shield it with a piece of cardboard or something similar.

Chances are, in the beginning, you will merely produce nervous squiggles without any meaning. But sooner or later, messages will come through.

It usually takes three or four sittings before the first intelligible results are achieved.

Don't prolong your sittings unduly, even after they do come. Be patient!

Expanding your group Once you have begun to produce results in your experiment, give up your solitary sittings and work with one or more other persons. For one thing, this considerably lessens the danger of fatigue or boredom, which may cause you to give up too early. Also, it is undeniable that two or three people can accomplish more than the single experimenter even during the period of preliminary training.

You must be certain, however, that you pick like-minded individuals to participate in your sessions.

For obvious reasons, you would not be likely to ask any friends who are hardnosed skeptics, who would not be able to recognize a miracle should one occur in their presence. At the other end of the pole, neither should you invite friends who are "true believers," who would hear a sign of the supernatural in every click of the thermostat.

It is most desirable to choose friends who have an interest in psychic development, a good deal of patience, and a rather well-established sense of balance.

The sender and the receiver Appoint one of you to be the sender (or transmitter), another the receiver (or recipient). Allow a third person to be the observer and recorder, alternating these roles among your group.

Suppose that you assume the role of the sender first. Seat yourself at a table, brightly lighted by a lamp placed somewhat behind you and shining directly on a piece of paper in front of you.

Turn your face toward the place where the receiver is seated, some distance away, with his back to you.

On a piece of paper before you, draw a simple figure, such as a circle, a cross, a triangle, and so forth. (For your early experiments it is wise to agree beforehand on four or five such basic designs to be transmitted.)

After drawing the figure, focus your attention upon it. Concentrate on it for a minute.

Then, mentally, *will* the recipient to receive the impression that you are transmitting.

The recipient, in turn, tries to keep his or her mind a blank. If he is also seated at a table with a piece of paper before him and a pencil in his hand, he may sketch the figures that he has mentally received from you. Once the impression is received, the recipient should draw it without hesitation, announcing when he or she has done so.

After some practice, you will achieve rather amazing results. You will find that the number of correct impressions received is much higher than they would be if they were mere guesses. You will see them stretch far beyond the laws of probability and chance.

Forming your spirit circle Once you have begun to work well together as a group, it will be time to form your spirit "Circle."

When such a decision has been reached, you will be joining a similar group of intimate friends and family members who, through the centuries, have met together to bridge the abyss that divides humankind from those who have gone above and beyond the physical.

Make it very clear that only those who are strongly intent upon establishing spirit communication should ever participate in your Circle. Seances are never to be a matter of an evening's fun and entertainment. It has often been observed by mediums that sympathy, earnestness, purpose, harmony, and patience are prerequisites to success in establishing spirit contact.

How many people should belong to a Circle is a matter of individual preference. Two people may produce excellent results if their psychic talents have been sufficiently developed.

Generations of experimentation have shown that four to six is a desirable number. Eight seems to be the maximum number of seekers for the preservation of harmony and the elimination of discord.

Private Circles usually meet in the home of one of the sitters. The room set aside for the seance should be medium sized, quiet, and removed as much as possible from street noises and other disturbances. It should be without a phone; nothing is more disruptive than the sudden ringing of the telephone bell.

The room should be well aired before the seance begins, and it should be comfortably warm but not overheated. Do not smoke during the actual session. The consumption of alcoholic beverages before and during the seance definitely should be banned.

Experience has shown that dry weather is best for the production of phenomena and that dampness or rain often hinders their occurrence. On the other hand, a sudden thunderstorm is very often conducive to the production of most unusual manifestations.

The best time for your Circle to meet is some time in the evening after dinner. You should choose a convenient hour when each of your sitters has had an opportunity to permit the day, with its worries and responsibilities, to have receded a bit into the background.

It is important that you sit regularly and always at the same time and place. Twice a week is the maximum number of seances for your Circle. A once a week meeting would be preferable.

Each individual seance should last no longer than an hour. In the beginning of your sittings, limit the sessions to about half an hour.

Seances are often exhausting. Especially during the early stages, when little or nothing occurs, they can become a great strain on every participant. Because of this fact, the sessions should not be overly extended, and you must be very cautious in your selection of participants. The impatient and the restless, the easily bored and the quickly distracted, must be excluded—regardless of how fond you may be of them in your more worldly interactions.

It should be understood from the very beginning that each person in your newly formed Circle must sit regularly and patiently for an absolute minimum of twelve seances. When you have completed the last session in the first cycle, permit the individuals to decide whether they care to continue studying and sitting with you.

Never restrain those members of the Circle who become

dubious and bored. Replace them with new sitters as soon as possible.

The first time that your Circle meets, select a leader to be in charge of the proceedings, to ask questions as soon as a spirit communicator manifests, and to time the sittings. It must be agreed by all that each sitter will obey the orders of the leader and abide always on his or her arrangements.

It might also be a good idea to appoint a secretary who will be responsible for recording each session and providing appropriate music.

The leader should assign seats around the seance table to members of the Circle. Once a seat has been assigned, it should be retained during the entire cycle of seances—unless unforeseen developments should make a change advisable.

The kind of intensity of light most appropriate for the development of spirit phenomena varies according to the psychic strength of the medium and the sitters. The best authorities on the subject consider it a kind of general rule that a bright white light is definitely detrimental to almost any kind of manifestation.

Seances by no means require complete darkness, but it is important that no direct light shines on the seance table.

Some Circles prefer sitting in darkness until the first unmistakable phenomenon occurs. From that point onward, a dim light is turned on.

All sitters should preserve a calm state of mind. It isn't necessary to be overly serious or to be gloomy; just be open-minded and relaxed.

Try to convince everyone that intense concentration should not be attempted. Tension, excitement, fear, nervousness—all can be as great a hindrance to the proceedings as arrogance, skepticism, and levity.

Wait patiently for what may happen. Don't be overly critical of what may manifest in those early stages. It is best in the beginning to accept what occurs, rather than to make immediate judgments and attempts to interpret.

Spiritual etiquette When spirit manifestations begin, be cordial to the entities. Welcome them warmly; speak to them confidently and calmly.

Prepare questions that you wish to ask beforehand. When answers come, do not flatly contradict them or declare that such things are impossible.

Later, when contact is firmly established, it will become possible to question the spirits and to ask them to define matters more completely.

All conversation with spirit entities should be carried on through the person chosen to direct the seance. Close adherence to this rule will not only prevent mix-ups and misunderstandings, but it will contribute greatly toward a more rapid progress in your Circle's development.

The messages you receive will vary greatly in value and content. Sometimes they will be absolutely startling, sometimes trifling, sometimes obviously transmitted in an attitude of teasing and gentle raillery.

The time that elapses before the first phenomenon occurs and the transmission of veridical messages (messages that can be substantiated and proved) will vary greatly from session to session.

On occasion, manifestations will start as soon as the lights are dimmed and the Circle closed. During other sittings, the participants may not be able to get beyond the simplest phenomena.

Almost certainly, though, results will get better and gain an importance from sitting to sitting. With the necessary patience and perseverance, some results will be absolutely certain to come through to you.

Choosing the medium After the first timid manifestations begin to occur, it may be desirable to establish who among you is the actual medium.

This can be easily accomplished by asking each member, in turn, to leave the room. The moment the real medium has been elminated from the Circle, the phenomena will cease.

It is possible, of course, that more than one of your number is mediumistic.

In itself, the matter is unimportant. By the time that your Circle arrives at the more complex experiments, the question of who is the best medium will have been answered in a dozen different ways. The less-powerful mediums—and all members of the Circle—will serve the principle medium as "batteries," enabling your Circle to produce increasingly impressive phenomena.

The trance state Trance is a completely natural and normal state. It comes about in psychically gifted persons in order to facilitate their communications with the world of spirit.

Since entranced people remember little or nothing of what takes place or of what they may say, it is important that the secretary of your Circle keep careful accounts of what has been uttered. Do not rely on memory.

Suppose that you are serving as the trance medium. Sit in the usual quiet seance room, holding hands with the person on either side of you. They, in turn, are holding hands with whomever is beside them, thus forming a circle around a table.

Sit for a moment or two listening to the restful music that should always be played during your sessions. Take a few deep breaths, holding them comfortably for a count of three.

Wait patiently.

Call out in a quiet voice whatever letters, words, images, symbols, or impressions begin to come to you. The secretary should be recording all utterances for later examination.

In all likelihood, your state of trance will become deeper with each word or image that comes to you. The heightened interest of the members of the Circle will give you additional psychic strength.

Messages will be delivered with increasing rapidity. Questions that your leader asks you to transmit to the spirit entities will be answered immediately. Additional phenomena may occur around you. All of these things will be signs that your mediumship, which may at first have been undeveloped and latent, is reaching a stage of continued progress.

The direct-voice sitting By the time that you and your Circle have reached the point where sittings for direct-voice manifestations can be held with reasonable expectation, it will have been definitely decided who among your group is the most gifted medium. When you hold your first direct-voice sitting, the seating arrangement should be different from the one that you have followed in all previous sessions.

The medium should occupy a chair set apart from the other sitters, who will now arrange themselves in a semicircle in front of him or her. No hand-chain is formed, unless the link-up is preferred by the members.

Play the usual meditative background music, and extinguish all lights. Sit quietly for a time or converse in low tones.

The medium should allow himself or herself to begin to enter the trance state. The Circle must remain patient and contemplative.

After a while, a whisper may be heard near the ear of one of the sitters. As soon as this occurs, the conversation and the music should stop. Expectant silence should prevail.

As in other seances, the sitters who are addressed by the voices should attempt to identify the spirit speakers. This is an easy enough task if the voice is a familiar one, such as that of a departed friend or a family member. If one should hear the voice of a stranger, it is now permissible to insist upon positive identification.

In direct-voice sittings, by the way, the sitters are permitted to ask questions of the spirit entities directly, rather than through the intercession of the leader of the Circle.

Direct-voice seances are best held in complete darkness. If the Circle decides that some illumination is preferred, select a colored bulb (or cover the bulb with a colored scarf or bit of gauze) that grants the most desired form of lighting.

Producing physical phenomena If there have been indications during your earliest sittings that one or another of your Circle may be developing the ability to produce physical phenomena, the leader of your group must instruct all members to observe strict rules of seance etiquette. It must be emphasized that at no time should the medium who is producing physical phenomena be touched during the trance state.

There are several tests to determine whether or not physical phenomena can manifest during one of your sittings.

During your table tilting, for example, try lifting your hands from the top of the table without breaking the circuit. If the table continues to move and to tap out answers, you may proceed with seances called for the express purpose of producing physical manifestations.

The same test holds true for Ouija board and planchette seances. Lift your fingertips off the planchette. If it keeps moving, you have a clear sign that you may proceed with seances for physical manifestations.

For a physical seance, place several small objects, such as a bell, various musical instruments, small trinkets, and so forth, on the table. There should also be some carbon paper or paper blackened with soot, together with clean white sheets, for possible spirit fingerprints. You may also supply putty, clay, or wax for impressions.

Many phenomena may occur. Light or heavy objects may be moved by unseen hands. The bell and musical instruments may be rung or played.

Sittings for partial or complete materializations require the same sort of conditions that are necessary at seances seeking physical phenomena. All white light should be eliminated. The forming of a circle is important once again. Music is desirable.

Physical and materializations seances frequently overlap. An object suddenly lifted off the table is seen to be carried by a materialized hand. A face may be seen under a musical instrument while it is being played.

Whatever happens, remain calm. Remember that no phenomenon is supernatural—only supernormal.

An altered-state technique to reach the other side Here is a guided meditation for establishing contact with the spiritual realm, which Frances and I have employed with great success. This method places the individual in an altered state of consciousness that enables him or her to reach out to accomplish a link-up with a guide or a more aware aspect of Self. Then, one may reach even farther and establish a contact with the world beyond death.

You may read the meditation, pausing now and then to ponder the significance of your inner journey and to receive elevation to that higher spiritual realm.

Or you may wish to read the techniques to another, permitting that individual to accomplish spiritual contact. Then, later on, that same friend may assist you in reaching a state of deep relaxation and assist you to establish your own link-up.

It is also possible to record your voice, reading these techniques into a tape cassette, so that you might play the tape back and allow your own voice to guide you through the relaxation process and through the heavenly realm.

Any of these methods can be effective. Your success depends upon your willingness to permit such an experience to manifest in your consciousness.

Imagine that you are lying on a blanket on a beautiful stretch of beach. You are lying in the sun or in the shade, whichever you prefer. You are listening to the rhythmic sound of the waves as they lap against the shore.

As you relax, you know that nothing will disturb you, nothing will distress you, nothing will molest you or bother you in any way. Even now, you are becoming aware of the golden light of love, wisdom, and knowledge that is moving over you, protecting you.

You know that you have nothing to fear. Nothing can harm you.

As you listen to the sound of the ocean waves, you feel all tension leaving your body. The sound of the waves helps you to become more and more relaxed.

You must permit your body to relax so that you may rise to higher states of consciousness. Your body must relax so that the real you may rise higher and higher to greater states of awareness.

You are feeling a beautiful energy of tranquility, peace, and love entering your feet; you feel every muscle in your feet relaxing.

That beautiful energy of tranquility, peace, and love moves up your legs, into your ankles, your calves, your knees, your thighs; and you feel every muscle in your ankles, your calves, your knees, your thighs relaxing, relaxing, relaxing.

If you should hear any sound at all—a slamming door, a honking horn, a shouting voice—that sound will not disturb you. That sound will help you to relax even more.

And now that beautiful energy of tranquility, peace, and love is moving up to your hips, your stomach, your back; you feel every muscle in your hips, your stomach, your back relaxing, relaxing, relaxing.

With every breath that you take, you find that your body is becoming more and more relaxed.

Now the beautiful energy of tranquility, peace, and love enters your chest, your shoulders, your arms, even your fingers; you feel every muscle in your chest, your shoulders, your arms, and your fingers relaxing, relaxing, relaxing.

And with every breath that you take, you find that you are becoming more and more relaxed.

Every part of your body is becoming free of tension. Every part of your body is becoming more and more relaxed.

Now that beautiful energy of tranquility, peace, and love moves into your neck, your face, the very top of your head, you feel every muscle in your neck, your face, and the very top of your head relaxing, relaxing, relaxing.

Your body is now relaxing, but your mind—your true self—is very aware.

And now, a beautiful golden globe of light is moving toward you. You are not afraid; you realize, you *know*, that within this golden globe of light is your guide.

Feel the love as this entity comes closer to you. Feel the vibrations of love moving over you—warm, peaceful, tranquil.

You feel love moving all around you. Two eyes are beginning to form in the midst of that golden light. The eyes of your guide! Feel the love flowing to you from your guide.

Now a face is forming. Oh, look at the smile on the lips of your guide. Feel the love that flows from your guide to you.

Now a body is forming. Behold the beauty of form, structure, and stature of your guide. *Feel* the love that flows to you from the very presence of your guide.

Your guide is now stretching forth a loving hand to you. Lift up your hand and accept your guide's hand into yours. *Feel* the love flowing through you. *Feel* the love as you and your guide blend and flow together in the Love Force.

Hand in hand, you feel yourself being lifted higher and higher. Your guide is taking you to the dimension of spirit. You are moving higher, higher, higher.

You are moving into a higher vibration.

You are moving toward a place of higher awareness, a heavenly realm.

Now you have arrived in that place. Look around you. The trees, grass, sky—*everything* is more alive here. The colors are more vivid.

You, too, have been transformed. It is as if you have a new nervous system: new eyes to see those things you have never before seen, new ears to hear what you have never before heard.

Look at the people coming to greet you. Look at their eyes. Feel the love. You recognize so many of them, dear ones from the Earth plane who have already come home.

They reach out to touch you, to embrace you, to kiss you. And you feel the love flowing all around you.

As you follow your guide through this heavenly realm, you feel love all around you. Love as you have never felt it on Earth. Love as you have yearned for it all of your life.

And as you stand there, bathed in love, some of those dear ones who have already come home are beginning to move closer to you. See them moving nearer.

Right now one of them is becoming very clear to you. You are beginning to recognize clearly who this person is. You remember instantly your relationship to this beautiful soul.

See the eyes, the mouth, the face, the body. You feel such joy moving through your essence. You are so happy to once again see this loved one.

You may now ask this loved one any question that you wish. The loved one may answer in words, in a series of gestures, or by presenting a symbol. Watch closely and listen, for your loved one is answering your question *Now:*

[Pause at this point to permit the spiritual answer to be received. If contact and questioning is desired with more than one loved one, the above may be repeated. If a dialogue is established between the seeker and the spirit entity, permit it to continue as long as it is productive. When the contact begins to fade or when the desired information is received, bring the seeker back to full consciousness using the method that follows.]

Now you must return to full consciousness in the physical realm of Earth. Do not sorrow. Know that you may return to this heavenly place again and again. You are never separated from your loved ones in the dimension of spirit. By maintaining the vibration of unconditional love in your life, you are always one with them, joined together in the Love Force.

At the count of five you will be returned to full consciousness. One . . . becoming awake. Two . . . becoming more and more awake, moving the fingers, making a fist. Three . . . becoming more and more awake, feeling very, very good in mind, body, and spirit. Four . . . becoming awake, feeling better than you have felt in weeks and weeks, months and months. Five . . . fully awake! Feeling great! Filled with unconditional love!

7

HAUNTED HOUSEHOLDS

The voice on the telephone was warped by confusion, tension, and fear. The young man, whom we shall call Jim, could not believe that such nightmarish experiences were actually occurring to him.

It had all begun for Jim and his fiancée Carol while he had been investigating UFO sightings in their home state. On one occasion Carol had accompanied Jim and other researchers. During the course of an evening's mysterious activities, she had somehow entered a trance-like state.

Later, in a strange dream, grotesque entities told Carol that they wanted her. She must leave Jim, for he was wrong for her, they said. If she did not join them, they would have Jim killed.

The dreams continued, becoming more violent and terrifying as the nights progressed.

One evening Carol was awakened from one of the nightmares by the ringing of her telephone. When she mumbled an answer, a harsh voice asked her if she was now ready to come over to *their* side.

The telephone became an instrument of fear for Carol. It rang at all hours, startling her with peculiar beeps and threatening voices that spoke in mechanical monotones.

Carol began to slip into trance more and more often. These trances were usually prefaced by a headache, a pain in the back of her neck, then a lapse of consciousness. As a trained nurse, Carol was able to recognize the symptoms of an approaching trance, but she seemed powerless to prevent its onset.

Jim and Carol had become engulfed in the living nightmare that psychical researchers and UFOlogists term the Men-in-Black (MIB) phenomenon. Briefly stated, the MIB is a phenomenon within a phenomenon, a strange blending of the UFO and poltergeist enigmas.

In several instances, men and women who have witnessed UFO activity—or related manifestations such as strange monsters, Bigfoot-type creatures, or bizarre phantom-like entities—have suffered a peculiar kind of personal harassment. Sinister voices whisper threats over the telephone and warn these witnesses to forget what they have seen. Eerie humanoid faces appear in the "snow" between television channels or on active channels after sign-off time and give instructions to the witnesses.

Often, these harassed witnesses receive visits from short, dark-complexioned men, usually three at a time, who threaten them and warn them to forget all thoughts of the phenomena that they have observed.

The MIB entities are described as having compelling eyes that are slanted in a manner somehow different from those of Orientals. Some witnesses have also mentioned slightly pointed or peculiarly misshapen ears. Others have stated that the MIB appeared to have difficulty speaking properly because of short-windedness, often gasping for breath in midsentence.

After a visit from the MIB entities, a witness's electrical utilities and appliances often become traitors in the mysterious employ of the sinister visitors. Telephones ring at all hours and bring threatening or nonsensically mechanical voices. Standard television or radio programming is interrupted by alien frequencies. Network video and audio are blotted out, to be replaced by the images of humanoids, who instruct the witnesses that they must cooperate with them.

Because he knew of my experience in dealing with poltergeists and other mysterious entities, Jim made a desperate long-distance telephone call to me to get my advice on how to free Carol from the apparent spell of the phenomenon.

First of all, I assured Jim that the MIB manifestations never appeared to be physically harmful. Frightening, threatening, indeed—but not actually harmful. Some witnesses had reported having suffered black or red eyes after an encounter, but that appeared to be connected with the peculiar electromagnetic aspect of the phenomenon.

The important thing, I told Jim, was not to play their game, and especially not to cast them in the role of evil entities. It is this dualistic concept that comes so readily to humankind that sets up the warfare structure with the phenomenon. If you permit hostility, then that is what you will receive.

In my opinion, the phenomenon is neither good nor evil. All such activity is the manifestation of a single source. How the MIB conduct themselves depends, in large part, on the human being with whom they interact.

In many ways, their effect is quite like that of an echo. Cry out in fear, and they'll give you good reason to fear them.

I am convinced that this aspect of the larger phenomenon has been constructed primarily as a teaching mechanism. Anyone who finds himself or herself a victim of the negative aspects of the phenomenon must at once begin restructuring reality, *excluding* the MIB entities and breaking their hold on his or her mental construct of what is real.

I sent Jim a letter in which I presented a number of specific guidelines for dissipating the poltergeistic activity that had been afflicting Carol.

My spoken and written advice seemed to provide Jim and Carol with the kind of support they needed, and the phenomenon around them appeared to decrease.

Satisfied that I had been able to assist Jim and Carol, I thought back to an earlier time when I had endured a number of poltergeistic plunderings of my own office.

One night as I had sat over my typewriter, I heard heavy footfalls at the top of the stairs. A quick glance told me that no one was there.

A favorite painting of Edgar Allan Poe fell to the floor. I became irritated.

Papers began to rustle off to my side. A single sheet became airborne.

I had had enough. A few nights before, several books had launched themselves from their shelves and had piled themselves up in the middle of the floor.

I looked up from my typewriter, rolled my eyes upward in disgust, and shouted: "Just cut it the hell out!"

Everything stopped.

I experienced that peculiar sensation one feels when he walks into a crowded, noisy room and everyone suddenly stops talking. I went back to my writing without further notice of anything but the work at hand.

It would seem that every kind of intelligence—regardless of how high or how low—wishes to be recognized. Nothing deters the activity of any thinking entity faster than ignoring it.

Of course I hadn't really ignored the invisible prowler. I had commanded the poltergeist-like force. I had refused to go along with its framework of reality, and my own change of attitude—from passive fear to rage—had apparently done the trick. I had served notice that I would no longer play the game.

The cessation of activity in my office had been so abrupt that it had been very much like the termination of some kind of lesson, some kind of testing process. Evidently, I had passed with satisfactory marks.

A few nights after I had last heard from Jim I received another panicked call from him. The force had returned. Even now it was thudding the walls of their apartment.

The long-distance line was able to transmit the sounds very clearly. Carol was whimpering in the background.

I kept repeating that they must remain calm. I assured them that they could stand firm against the phenomenon and resist it. I told them over and over not to show fear, not to play the game.

At last the terrible sounds ceased. Things were calm and quiet once again in Jim's apartment. Carol came on an extension, and they both thanked me for my help in negating the energy.

I cradled the phone, feeling rather pleased with myself. I leaned back in my chair and reached for the book I had been reading.

Thud! Thud! The first hammering sounds came from the ceiling. *Thud! Thud!* The next blows vibrated the wall near a bookcase.

The poltergeistic energy had traveled along the telephone line and was now manifesting in my office. Somehow, the frequency of the disturbances had been transmitted well over a thousand miles.

Several books began to dislodge themselves from their shelves. The powerful thudding sounds seemed to echo from wall to wall.

I must confess that it took every ounce of my mental resolve and my emotional reserve to stay in that office during the first few moments of the sudden and unexpected poltergeistic onslaught. My mind boggled at the thought that the chaotic energy had used the telephone system to transport itself from Jim's apartment to my office.

I practiced a bit of yogic breathing to calm myself, then I told myself that I must practice what I had been preaching to Jim and Carol. I must refuse to play the game. I must assert my control of the situation. I must not show fear.

When I left my office later that evening, the disturbances had ceased. With great effort of will, I had held my psychic ground.

And it appears that the poltergeistic energy had spent itself, for I received no more distressful telephone calls from Jim and Carol.

From the outside, the old farmhouse was magnificent. It was a solid two-story dwelling with an inviting front porch that sat atop a grassy hill. It was flanked by majestic pines and backed by a dwindling number of oak and walnut trees that soon surrendered to a cornfield. At the foot of the hill was a picturesque, meandering creek with a small but sturdy bridge. Across the lane from the barn was a cabin said to be one of the very oldest pioneer homes in the county. Yes, from the outside, the sturdy Iowa farmhouse seemed an ideal home in which our family might attempt an experiment in country living.

From the inside, however, it seemed another matter entirely. I first entered the home with a friend who is very psychically sensitive. "Someone died here," he stated bluntly as soon as we crossed the threshhold into the dining room.

The woman whose home we were in the process of purchasing appeared startled by my friend's immediate announcement. When he quickly added, "A man died in the room across from the kitchen," she became visibly upset.

Within moments, we had the whole story. Papa, her father, had, in his day, been a well-respected church and community leader. His "day" had been in the 1920s and 1930s, and he had steadily grown more reclusive and more strongly opposed to modern technology. Papa's distrust of modern times extended to storm windows, electric lights, and running water. Life with Papa had been a rugged existence.

He had yielded to electric lights sometime in the 1940s, and he had loved to sit in his room and listen to the radio—one of his few concessions to the contemporary world around him. He had not permitted running water in his house during his lifetime, and the plumbing that we now saw in the house had been only recently installed. There still was no drinking water in the home, however, and if we did not wish to carry buckets from the spring near the barn, we would have to drill a well.

My objections to the farmhouse were outvoted, and we were soon moving to the country to inhabit Papa's monument to the "good old days." I strongly felt a presence in the home, and I was concerned about the children, for the presence I detected did not seem to be a hospitable one.

I should state firmly at this point that moving into a home with an unseen resident held no terrors for me, personally. I had grown up in a farm home in which we had continued paranormal manifestations, ranging from knockings, rappings, the sound of measured footsteps, and occasional materializations.

Among my earliest childhood memories are the man and woman who would walk into my bedroom at night and stand looking down at me. The man wore a black suit and seemed of rather stern demeanor. The woman wore an old-fashioned dress with lace at the collar. Assessing their appearance from photographs that I saw in an old album when I was older, they were quite likely my great-grandparents, who had dwelt in the farmhouse long before my birth.

The dimension of spirit had always been very much a part of my mother's life. She permitted my sister and me to perceive the eerie occurences as evidence that, from time to time, a greater reality can impinge upon our more limited physical reality.

As I evaluated the present situation, we had a problem. If we truly were dealing with the earthbound spirit essence of a man who had been a pious church leader and a fervent opponent of progress, just how would he take to a family moving into his home that was headed by a psychical investigator and by four kids who would immediately begin playing stereos and television sets? And how would the impressionable psyches of the kids, aged sixteen to eight, respond if the spirit became antagonized?

I was the first to undergo an initiation at the hands of an invisible welcoming committee.

I was alone in the house on a Sunday morning having some tea and toast while I read the newspaper. One moment things were as idyllic as they could be, the next my tranquility was shattered by a violent explosion that seemed to come from the basement.

Fearing that the oil-burning furnace had somehow exploded, I opened the basement door, expecting the worst. I could hear what seemed to be the walls of stone and brick caving in on the washer, the dryer, and the other appliances. I expected to be met by billowing clouds of thick, black smoke.

But the instant I stepped onto the basement landing, all sounds of disturbances ceased. The furnace was undamaged. The walls stood firm and solid. There was no smoke or fire.

Before I could puzzle the enigma through, I was startled by the sound of yet another explosion coming from somewhere upstairs. I had a terrible image of the old brick chimney collapsing; then I was pounding my way up the stairs.

The attic was as serene as the basement had been. I shook my head in confusion as I studied the sturdy beams and the excellent workmanship that held the roof and the brick chimney firmly erect and braced. The house had been built by master carpenters and bricklayers. It could probably withstand a tornado, I thought to myself as I attempted to understand what was happening around me.

A massive eruption sounded from the basement again, creating the visual image of several hand grenades being triggered in rapid succession.

I slammed the attic door behind me, fearing the awesome damage that must surely have occurred.

But before I could run back down the stairs to inspect the extent of the destruction, I heard what sounded like someone tap-dancing behind the door to my son Steven's room. I knew that Steven did not tap dance. I knew that I was alone home.

Then I thought of Reb, our beagle. I laughed out loud in

relief. The sound of "tap-dancing" was the clicking of the dog's paws on the wooden floor.

But why wasn't Reb barking to be released? He was never shy about expressing his wishes, frustrations, or irritations.

I hesitated with my hand on the doorknob. I felt an even greater hesitation when I heard Reb barking outside. The dog was at the back door by the kitchen. I had been so engrossed in the mystery of the strange disturbances that I had forgotten that I had let the beagle out. It was cold that morning and Reb was barking to come into the warm house.

Who—*what*—was still merrily dancing behind the door to Steven's room?

I shamed myself for permitting atavistic fears to stay my hand. I twisted the knob and pushed open the door.

The room was empty. And the dancing stopped as suddenly as had the explosions when I had swung aside the basement and attic doors.

I suddenly felt as though I were being scrutinized by a dozen or more pairs of eyes.

Another detonation roared up at me from the basement.

I sensed a game plan behind all of this. I was now supposed to dash down the stairs in puzzled panic, desperately seeking the cause of the violent "explosion." I could almost hear the anticipatory giggles of unseen pranksters.

I resolved not to play the silly game anymore. I walked purposefully back to the kitchen table where I had left my tea, toast, and Sunday newspaper.

It sounded as if the attic roof was being torn from its anchoring beams. The basement walls shuddered and collapsed in what seemed to be another explosion.

During my career as a psychical researcher, I had become well versed in the games that certain entities liked to play with people. I decided to do my best to ignore the phenomena.

The tap-dancing was nearer now. It was coming from the music room, the room that the previous owners had kept locked and unused—Papa's room. I had placed the piano, television, and stereo in the room and had repainted the walls and the ceiling. I had blessed the room and announced that it would henceforth be a place of love and laughter.

I was determined not to glance up from my newspaper, even if Papa, a headless horseman, or a snarling troll came walking out of the music room. I was not going to play the game.

Within about twenty minutes, the disturbances had quieted themselves. I was relieved that I had guessed the secret. It appeared that the invisible pranksters did not enjoy playing tricks on someone who remained indifferent to such a grand repertoire of mischief.

Because I did not wish to alarm the rest of the family and because I was totally immersed in working on a new book at my office in the city, I did not mention the incident to anyone.

Then, about three nights later, when I was working late at my office, I received an urgent telephone call from my older son, Bryan. The panic in the sixteen-year-old's voice told me that I must drive out to the farmhouse at once.

When I arrived, I found Bryan barricaded in his room, together with Reb and a .12-gauge shotgun. After I had calmed the boy, I learned that Bryan, too, had fallen victim to the tricksters.

Bryan had been alone at home watching television in the music room. He had heard what he assumed to be the sound of other family members returning. He listened to the familiar noises of an automobile approaching, car doors slamming, voices and laughter, and the stomping of feet on the front porch.

Then he had been surprised to hear loud knocking at the front door. Everyone in the family had his or her own key, so why should anyone knock? And why should they be pounding at the front door when they usually entered through the kitchen's back door?

Bryan begrudgingly stirred himself from his television program and went to admit whoever was at the front porch.

He was astonished to find it empty.

Just as he was about to step outside in an attempt to solve the mystery, he heard knocking at the back door. Uttering a sigh of frustration, Bryan slammed the door and began to head for the kitchen.

He had taken no more than a few steps when the knocks were once again at the front door.

By now Bryan knew that someone was playing a joke on him. He turned on the yard light so that he could identify the jokesters' automobile. He gasped when he saw that his was the only car on the farm.

Fists were now thudding both doors. And Reb was going crazy, growling and baring his teeth.

Bryan next became aware of an eerie babble of voices and short bursts of laughter. And someone very large was definitely leaning against the kitchen door, attempting to force it open.

That was when he had called me; and a few seconds of hearing my son's strained, frightened voice and the angry snarls of the dog in the background convinced me that something was very wrong.

"Dad," Bryan told me, "Reb and I are in my room. Someone is coming up the stairs one step at a time. I can hear him move up one step at a time!"

An intuitive flash informed me what was occurring. The invisible pranksters were playing games again.

"Bry, your fear is feeding it," I advised my son. "It has already tried the game with me. Try to stay calm. Put on some music. Distract your mind. I'm on my way home right now!"

It had snowed earlier that day, and I prayed for no ice and no highway patrolmen. I was fortunate in both respects, and I managed to shave off four minutes from the normal twelve-minute drive to the farmhouse.

The doors were still locked from the inside, and Bryan was still barricaded in his room with Reb. I offered silent thanks that the boy hadn't blown any holes in himself or the walls with the shotgun.

I showed Bryan that there were no footprints in the freshly fallen snow. There was no evidence of tire tracks in the lane. No human agency had visited him, I explained, but, rather, some nonphysical intelligences who would initiate a spooky game with anyone who would play along with them.

Early the next evening, I gave my children instructions on how best to deal with any ghostly mechanisms of sound or sight that might frighten them.

Basically, the strategy was to remain as indifferent and as aloof to the disturbances as possible. In a good-natured way, one should indicate that he or she simply did not wish to play such silly games.

Under no circumstances should one become defiant or angry or threatening. The laws of polarity would only force the tricksters into coming back with bigger and spookier tricks in response to the negative energy that had been directed toward them.

Whether we were dealing with poltergeists, restless limbo spirits, or a repository of unknown energy that somehow mimicked human intelligence, I felt that I had given the kids some advice that was sound.

Bryan had experienced the phenomenon firsthand, so he was now better prepared to confront it should the situation arise. Steven had already intellectualized the occurrences and found them fascinating. Kari, who had strong mediumistic abilities, seemed aware of the disturbances, but remained strangely aloof from them.

It was all a little too awesome for eight-year-old Julie to sort into her reality, however. Whenever she was left alone in the farmhouse the entities would gang up on her, and I would return to find her standing at the end of the lane or seeking refuge in a neighbor's home. In each instance she complained of having heard strange voices, laughter, and weird music.

One night, just as I entered my office, I heard the telephone ringing. It was Julie. She had been calling the office ever since I had left home. She was in tears. A dramatic manifestation had begun within minutes after I had left her at the kitchen table eating cookies and drinking milk.

I cradled the telephone, locked the office, and returned home. Julie was waiting for me at the end of the lane.

This time it had begun with laughter from the music room. There was a noisy blur of voices, as if several people were trying to speak at once. Then came some "funny piano music" and the sound of a drum.

Valiantly, Julie had tried to practice what I had told her to do: Remain calm; act aloof. Don't play the game with whatever it is that likes to play such spooky tricks on people.

When the rhythmic tapping of the drum suddenly gave way to blaring horns and trumpets, Julie's indifference melted.

I had not been gone for more than two or three minutes, but Julie knew that I was headed for the office. She just let the telephone ring until I answered it.

Not long ago Julie, now nineteen, and I recalled the incidents that she had experienced in the eerie old farmhouse from the vantage point of our home in Scottsdale, Arizona. Interestingly enough, Julie had only recently identified the music that she had heard coming from the music room on several occasions when she had been left alone. She said:

> *Some girlfriends and I were just driving around one night, and we had on one of those radio stations that play nostalgic music from the "good old days." We were talking about how different some of the music used to be, when suddenly I just about freaked out. It was a good thing that I wasn't driving! I heard some of the music that I had heard coming from that spooky room, and all those terrible memories came back to me.*

Julie had heard Glen Miller's "In the Mood."

Incredibly, it had been music from the 1940s that had driven Julie from the house. Whenever she hears a Benny Goodman, a Duke Ellington, or a Glenn Miller piece, she has to leave the room, for it was their old records that she had heard playing from the darkened recesses of the music room.

Although she grew up in a home where eclectic musical tastes were enjoyed, I must confirm that the tunes of the 1940s would have been foreign to Julie at that time of her life. The family had classical, folk, motion picture themes, rock, pop, and Broadway show tunes, but we had no big-band sounds from the 1940s in our collection.

Now that she was older, I shared with Julie what I knew about the music room. Papa had been a strong-willed man who didn't care much for progress—not even running water in the house. And he never would have approved of his daughter and her husband selling the place. He had died in that room, and they had kept it locked. They had never used it again while they lived there. Things just hadn't felt right in there.

Papa might not have cared much for most of the instruments of progress, but he must have accepted radio. And he probably tolerated the music of the 1940s, the years when he would have been participating in some of the most meaningful experiences in his life.

Or maybe the invisible tricksters just loved to jitterbug.

Or maybe Julie had been somehow listening to radio broadcasts from the past.

Before we compile a list of anymore "maybe's," let us

remember what so many great metaphysical teachers have advised us: The surest protection against chaotic entities is to strive always to walk in balance and to love unconditionally all living things.

I first heard of the bloody basement in Lincoln, Nebraska, from a reporter on the *Lincoln Journal and Star*. The image of a bearded man with long, unkempt hair was often seen coming through a wall. Then what appeared to be blood would ooze from the walls and pour from the faucets near the washing machine.

The man was thought to be the spirit form of the angry husband who had murdered his wife and her lover with shotgun and knife in a darkened back room of the basement. The manifestation of blood was the silent commemoration of the violent deed.

When I arrived on the scene with the well-known Chicago medium, Irene Hughes, the family had refused to use their basement any longer. The haunting had the mother, and especially the teenaged daughter, on the edge of hysteria.

As the medium, members of the family, and I stood in that eerie back room, my associate Glenn McWane and the reporter observed a strange phenomenon. The door kept trying to close on us.

"See there?" Glenn pointed out. "From the angle in which the door is set, it should naturally swing open. The floor slants a bit, and it would be an uphill fight against gravity for the door to close by itself."

But the door had been swinging closed.

On two occasions, as the journalist was trying to take a picture of us in the back room, the door had swung nearly shut and had ruined his shot.

Another time, Glenn had wedged his toe under the door to hold it open, and it had nearly bent at the top because there had been so much pressure exerted against it.

"All right," I said after Irene had finished receiving impressions from the room. "Shut the darned door if that's what it wants so badly."

Glenn swung the door to the jamb, then found that he had to lift it to make a tight fit. "Now the blame thing should be happy," he said, grinning. "It's closed good and tight."

With the troublesome door firmly closed, we moved to join the others, who were walking toward the other end of the basement, where the image of a baby's face had been set into the wall. It was here that Melody, the teenaged daughter, felt that death awaited any trespasser.

"Don't permit yourself to become hysterical," Mrs. Hughes said in her soft voice. "You'll only give strength to whatever negative forces might possibly be harbored somewhere in this house."

After Irene Hughes had pacified the family about the evil effects of the basement, we walked upstairs to the daughter's room.

"Do you often feel that someone is peeking in that window at you?" she asked Melody.

"All the time!" the teenager shuddered in instant agreement. "It's such an icky feeling!"

Irene moved to a dresser. "There's a strange, almost electrical vibration here," she said.

"We've felt it in the same spot," Mrs. Richard, our frightened hostess, confirmed. "Several friends have felt the same thing there."

"It feels like something moving underneath me," Irene said.

"We've felt it for six years now," Mrs. Richard said as she dabbed at the corners of her mouth with a handkerchief.

Just then we were all startled by a loud pounding sound from the basement. It sounded as though a door had been slammed open and something very heavy and very angry was coming up the stairs.

BAM! BAM! BAM!

"It's right under me!" Mrs. Hughes shouted. "It's like somebody pushing, banging up the floor. Did everyone feel it . . . hear it?"

We would have to have lost feeling below our knees and have gone deaf not to have felt and heard the powerful series of knocks.

Glenn and the reporter were already on their way down to the basement. I knew where they were heading, and I walked back to the head of the stairs and shouted down at them: "Well?"

Glenn called up that the door to the back room, the scene of the grisly shotgun deaths, was wide open. It appeared that we could not "tame" the presence in the room that easily. And it refused to be locked in by a puny door.

When the two men rejoined us, the journalist said that he had felt a "force" push past him just seconds before the pounding had begun on the floor. After he had vocalized this admission, others who had been standing in line with the basement stairway said that they, too, had felt "something" rush by them.

127

Irene told us that she was "getting" another image of the spirit in the basement. "He was seen in a mirror once," she said, "and the mirror was broken."

"That happened to me," Melody spoke up, a tremor slightly warping her voice. "I saw the guy standing behind me when I was combing my hair. He was so ugly that I just smashed the mirror."

Irene continued with her impressions, telling us that the spirit was that of a tall man who was not as ugly as he was unkempt.

Mrs. Richard reentered the conversation by saying that they had often seen the man's shadow. "That shadow was the first thing that we ever saw out of the ordinary in this house. We saw a man's shadow, his outline, in this doorway."

The first time the specter had appeared, Mrs. Richard had thought it to be her husband coming home from work. "I kept calling his name, and he didn't answer me. I thought he was doing something just to frighten me."

Melody said that seeing the shadow was a terrible experience. "Every time we see that shadow, I know it is that big, ugly man trying to get us, trying to pull us into the grave with him!" she said.

Irene left the girl's bedroom to walk to the kitchen sink. "There is another man that you see sometimes when you are doing dishes," she said to Mrs. Richard.

The woman admitted that the medium's impression was correct. "Yes, it's a frightening presence to me. Whenever I feel him next to me, I run out the door. I can't stay anywhere in this house for too long when I am alone."

Irene told her not to be frightened of this particular spirit. "This man is someone who has passed over and who belongs to you. He wants to come through to you. Because you do not understand these things, you have only fear when you sense his presence.

"This is not the man in the basement," Irene emphasized. "This feels like a very different person. This feels more like your father."

Mrs. Richard said that her father had been deceased since 1959, adding that "there have been times before a crisis when I have felt his presence."

The medium left the kitchen and walked to a smaller room near the front door. She told us that she felt a "fast heartbeat" in this place. "This was the room of the man who was stabbed to death in the basement."

Mrs. Richard reported that this was the room in which they had seen a moving light on some evenings. "We have never been able to explain the light as being caused by any kind of reflection or any light source that we can identify," she said. "It moves across the room from the picture on the wall, to the window, to that light fixture over there."

Irene informed us that this had once been the victim's bedroom. Mrs. Richard confirmed that the room had been used as such before the Richard family moved in.

> *I feel that his spirit considers this house his home and that is why he keeps returning here. That is why you have seen his image coming out of the wall. That is why you have seen his shadow in the doorway as if he were coming home from work. And the blood pouring from the faucets is a reminder of the terrible way in which he was murdered. But please understand, this spirit means no one any harm.*

After Irene offered a prayer and a meditation for the restless entity's peace of spirit, we left the house to enter a garage in the Richards' back yard. It was here, according to most reports, that the maddened husband had put a violent end to his wife with a shotgun blast. The room in the basement, the journalist clarified for us, was where the body had been dragged. It was a separate crime that had resulted in the stabbing of a man in the same back room where the mangled wife had been deposited by her husband. Irene offered another prayer for all troubled entities that may have been drawn to the scene of terrible death.

The Richard house, in my opinion, was a kind of "psychic supermarket" with an extraordinarily wide range of phenomena coexisting within its walls. There was the strange door that would not stay either open or closed; there was the ghost of the unkempt man that had appeared in the back room of the basement and in the girl's bedroom; there was the "blood" that had flowed from the faucet in the basement; there was the thumping, thudding "force" that had jarred all of us in the girl's bedroom.

Irene Hughes left the Richards with instructions as to how they might employ psychic self-defense against any unwanted spectral visitors, and she gave the mother and the daughter private consultations designed to fortify them against the fear and hysteria that had begun to warp their perspective toward life in the old house.

Although the Richard house was basically a haunted one, there were certainly strong elements of poltergeistic-psychokinetic manifestations involved. The disturbed teenager, so often an essential ingredient in poltergeist manifestations, was present, but then so were the possibilities of virulent memory patterns having been impressed upon the environment by two murders. The mother and her daughter felt a definite interaction with at least two spirit entities, and Irene seemed to sense them and describe them exactly as the women had seen them.

PLAGUED BY THE POLTERGEIST

Although the poltergeist, that racketing bundle of projected repressions, is usually associated with the youth entering puberty and defining his or her sex role, such psychokinetic disturbances as the levitation of crockery and furniture and the materialization of voices and forms have been reported among newlyweds and lovers during their period of adjustment.

The late psychoanalyst Dr. Nandor Fodor believed that the human body is capable of releasing energy in an unconscious and uncontrolled manner, thereby providing the power for the poltergeist's pranks. Author Sacheverell Sitwell agreed that the psychic energy for such disturbances usually comes from the psyche of someone undergoing sexual trauma.

"The particular direction of this power is always toward the secret or concealed weaknesses of the spirit . . . the obscene or erotic recess of the soul," Sitwell conjectured.

A female medium told me that she was capable of producing more phenomena when she was sexually frustrated. "Materializations, for example," she said. "I can produce stronger materializations and make them last longer if I am sexually frustrated or if I have become sexually aroused. I find it more difficult to conduct an effective seance if I am satisfied sexually, although sometimes during an especially good seance, I will reach orgasm as I am producing a materialization.

You [the author] generally see the poltergeist as a psychological phenomenon. I can agree with this theory, but I also believe that sexual frustration and longing, and two kids trying to adjust to marriage, or sex, can attract entities in many different forms. I do agree with you privately—although I would probably deny it publicly—that there is a strong link between sex and psychic phenomena.

If two young people who are experimenting with the regenerative life force and learning to adjust to each other's sexual desires and needs are truly transmitting all sorts of powerful vibrations, then it might seem within the realm of possibility that certain of these life-force waves might in some way reactivate old memory patterns that have permeated "haunted" rooms. At the same time, these sensual shock waves might stimulate the activity of certain shadowy entities best left undisturbed.

Leona J. told me of an experience that happened to her and her fiancé shortly before their marriage in 1932. They had gone to a movie, then decided to drive out to the tiny house in the country where they would live after they had celebrated their nuptials.

It was fun to go there and plan our future. The house was on land that was too wooded to be good farmland, but we planned to plant only a small garden, and Karl would continue his job in town.

We had only kerosene lamps in those days, but they always gave off such a cheery light—at least, they usually did. That night, when Karl lit the lamp, I had an eerie feeling that something was wrong, that we were not alone. Karl must have felt the same way as I did, because he kept looking over his shoulder like he expected to catch sight of someone spying on us.

"I'm going to have a look around," he said, trying to sound casual. He took the lamp, so I stayed right beside him. We walked through the small house, and Karl grinned at me sheepishly, as if he were apologizing for feeling uneasy in what was to be our honeymoon cottage.

We heard a strange chattering, like some giant squirrel or chipmunk, coming from a dark corner in the room. It sounded unreal, unearthly, and a strange coldness passed over my body. "Let's go, Karl," I whispered. "I'm frightened."

Before we could move toward the door, Karl suddenly threw his hands up over his head as if he were trying to grab something behind him. His head seemed pulled backward and to one side. His mouth froze in a grimace of pain and fear, and his eyes rolled wildly. He lost balance, fell to his knees, then to his side. He kicked over a chair as he rolled madly, fighting and clawing the air around his neck.

I stood by helplessly, stunned with fear and bewilderment. Karl managed to struggle to his feet. His eyes bulged and he gasped fiercely for each breath. Some unseen thing seemed to be strangling him.

"The door . . . open . . . run to car . . . you drive," he panted. We ran to the car, Karl stumbling, staggering as if something heavy and strong were perched atop his shoulders with a death grip about his throat. "I . . . can't get . . . damned thing off!"

I got behind the wheel of the car. "Drive . . . fast!" Karl said, his hands desperately trying to pry the invisible monster's paws from his throat.

I drove for about two miles down the road. Suddenly there was a blinding flash inside the car. A brilliant ball of fire about the size of a basketball shot ahead of our car, then veered sharply to the left and disappeared into a clump of trees.

I did not stop all the way back to town. Karl lay gasping beside me, his head rolling limply on the back of the seat. He did not speak until we were back inside the city limits. "It was some inhuman thing from the pits of hell," he said. "It was big, strong, and it would have killed me."

Leona J. concluded her account by writing that, although they returned to their small home with some trepidation, they never again encountered that monstrous, invisible strangler that chattered like a giant rodent.

ENCOUNTERING RESTLESS SPIRITS

Are there really such things as restless spirits who wander between dimensions of reality in some kind of limbo world?

During my more than quarter century as a psychical researcher, I have become much more open to such concepts as viable explanations of some of the eerie and remarkable phenomena I have witnessed. Since I am now married to a woman who seems to have access to such in-between worlds and to the farther reaches of the cosmos, I have many times asked her to share her insights regarding such mysterious matters.

Frances has said that to understand poltergeists, ghosts, and so forth, we must always remember that all is energy in various stages and levels of reality.

Within the vibrational frequencies of the Mother-Father Creator, there exist only the most harmonious and the highest of all creative energies. The farther an entity moves away from such a level, the more chaotic and destructive its energies become.

Frances understands the Divine Plan as one in which the Creator desired to expand, increase in complexities, and to experience life in myriad forms and dimensions. This impulse was guided into being, and the patterned energies resulted in the creation of all things.

We are reflections of the Creator. We are electromagnetic systems of energy—spiritually, mentally, physically.

We can also create electromagnetic energy. Our mind-brain units produce energies that not only affect the musculature of our bodies and prompt them to enact our thoughts, but also cause manifestations on other levels of reality.

So it is, Frances emphasizes, that our very thoughts can be creative or destructive. Repressed and expressed negative energies can wreak havoc on our total being. Creative thoughts can bring harmony to us on every level of our spiritual, mental, and physical selves.

We have a spirit within our being that occupies our body. The spirit is connected to our body by an electromagnetic current that remains intact until the transition time known to us as physical death.

Depending on our thoughts and our interactions with all of life, our spirit within vibrates with either high, harmonious energies or low, chaotic energies.

When we think and act in ways that are filled with love, we are in harmony with the Divine Plan and we generate energies that elevate our being. But when we think and act in ways that are filled with hate or apathy, our spirit, mind, and body vibrate with chaotic, low emanations.

Frances' guidance told her that there are various levels of spiritual reality, which range from the highest to the lowest. The highest, most harmonious levels are known to humankind as the Heavenly Realm. The lowest, most chaotic levels are called Hell. The levels in between constitute Limbo.

There are many vibrational levels of limbo, some of which are closer to the heavenly vibration, others of which are closer to the chaotic realms.

Physical death is a process whereby one's body begins to lose the ability to manufacture electromagnetic energy and begins to vibrate at a very low frequency—thus separating from the higher vibrations of spirit within the fleshly shell until the electromagnetic current that connects spirit and body no longer exists. When a person dies, the spirit within continues to vibrate at whatever the level of spiritual awareness before the moment of physical death. As the fleshly shell falls away, the spirit is free to enter the frequency nearest its own rate of vibration.

The spirit of a person who has done his or her best to live in accordance with the Divine Plan vibrates at a high frequency. Those spirits who vibrate with low, disharmonious, chaotic vibrations as a result of having lived lives of disorder, confusion, and hate-filled unproductivity vibrate at a low frequency.

There is no death, only a change of worlds, only a transition of energies. Where there was once spirit, mind, and body, there now exists only spirit and mind.

Within the realm of limbo, all manner of spirits may be found. Some are merely bewildered, uncertain as to what occurred to them when death came. Others are still so attached to people or places on the Earth plane that they try not to leave material existence.

Those spirits in the lowest regions of limbo are often filled with anger at finding themselves in the horrible domain of their own making. They try in every way to affect and to influence the minds and lives of all those living persons who will receive them. They wish to possess the living so that they might escape the hell of their creation. Many horrible crimes have occurred because of contact with these evil spirits, and it is these entities who are referred to as "demons" or "devils" from hell.

Whenever people lose control of their minds and their

bodies—such as through immoderate use of alcohol or drugs—they recklessly open themselves to contact with the realm of the chaotic and the lost spirits.

Never forget, Frances reminds us, that all is vibration, all is energy. Both the drugged human and the limbo spirits are operating at a low level of vibration. It is, therefore, easy for them to become in tune with each other.

In like manner, she warns, when anyone, even while in an undrugged state, goes about his or her daily activities in low vibrations emanating from hateful, distorted, chaotic thoughts, that person has made himself or herself vulnerable to contact with an entrapped spirit from the low, chaotic levels of vibration. Tragically, many people have already established such contact and remain unaware of it.

Because our minds are sending and receiving instruments that operate on electromagnetic energies, we can, on occasion, "tune in" to another's mental energies, be they living or dead. Communication with the physically dead is possible, Frances states, because the mind and spirit survive the death of the flesh and the mental energies continue to function.

She strongly advises everyone to practice unconditional love toward all living things so that one's levels of vibratory contact will always be of the highest. When we practice the proper types of meditation, our minds can soar free of our bodies, and, depending on our vibratory rate, we can be in touch with beings from beyond space and time.

Even those who seek contact only with the realm of higher vibrations, where angelic beings and spirits of the highest order exist, must remember that our physical world is closer to the lower, more chaotic frequencies. Because we exist in a material world, the vibrations of humankind are nearer the lower vibratory realm than the higher, spiritual realm. It is, therefore, easier to make contact with the chaotic entities in the lower realms.

Many of the entities in limbo desperately try to contact the people of Earth to warn them of what may lie beyond or to attempt to set the record straight in regard to the occurrences of their own lives. Many merely need to be heard so that they can be relieved of their desire to relay some information and get on with the process of elevating their energies to a higher realm.

The spirits in the regions of limbo can learn and elevate

themselves, but it is a much harder task than while living on Earth. Spiritual advancement in limbo must be assisted by entities from the higher realms or by sensitive men and women from the physical world who send them thoughts of love.

Frances tells us that we should not be overly concerned about making *unwanted* contact with chaotic spirits. Remember those words of advice given in Scriptures: "By their fruits, you shall know them. If they speak of good and of God, then they are from God. Satan does not divide against himself or he shall perish."

When you are in communication with an enlightened being from the higher spiritual realms, you will feel yourself being bathed in the highest expression of love that you have ever known. In her book of universal truths and channeled teachings, *Reflections from an Angel's Eye*, Frances assures us: "You will experience a oneness with all things, and love will become one with you. You will know no fear or apprehension from such an encounter."

If you should interact with a spirit being from the higher regions of limbo, you will feel a much lesser love and peace surrounding you.

If you should confront an entity from the chaotic realms, the lower levels of limbo, you will feel at once a prickling sensation that will seem to crawl over your entire being. You will instantly become filled with ever-increasing doubt that will soon turn to mounting terror, depending on the strength of the discordant vibrations emanating from the contacting spirit.

If you should ever make contact with such a chaotic, evil being, utter prayers and blessings of love. Fill your entire essence with unconditional love for all things, including the communicating spirit.

Then create in your mind the clear picture of your closing a door. Concentrate on this image. Focus on that picture in your mind. The image of closing a door will symbolize that you are shutting off that particular contact and blocking that spirit from you.

Speak not to it, Frances admonishes. Do not listen to it and it will go to find someone else of lower vibrations who will be more receptive to it.

In order to prevent contact with the confused or raging, entrapped entities of darkness, you must practice loving all living things unconditionally, for therein lies the power of the highest and the true energy of the Creator. When your spirit within vibrates with the highest form of love, when your purpose in living is to exist in harmony with the Divine Plan, you will make contact only with those spirits who are in the realm known as heaven. You will establish communication with the angelic beings and you will receive love, wisdom, and knowledge.

"Interacting with spiritually evolved beings is the most beautiful, beneficial experience that one can enjoy while still in the physical embodiment of flesh," Frances announces. "Such contacts will also establish your eternal happiness as well, for you will be enlightened with the most harmonious of vibrations."

8

JEALOUS SPIRITS THAT WON'T LET GO

Not very long ago one of my correspondents sent me a report containing the reminiscences of a friend's grandfather, who had suffered an attack from a possessive spirit.

The man's wife had died very young, leaving the Kentucky farmer with a number of small, motherless children. Before her death, however, the wife had warned her husband that she would not rest peacefully if he took another woman to his bed. The husband had promised his dying wife that this would not be so; but after a year of attempting to be both father and mother to his children, as well as trying to scratch a living out of the soil, the farmer decided that he must take another wife.

There was neither time nor money for the traditional honeymoon when he took his new bride in 1936, so the newlyweds simply drove from the church to the man's farm.

As she prepared the bed that night, the bride took a lovely quilt from a cabinet and smoothed it across the rather worn bedspread.

"You gonna use that quilt on the bed?" the farmer asked, trying to mask his discomfort.

"Why, yes," his bride replied. "It's so beautiful. What intricate work. Who made it?"

"It . . . it's been in the family," the man mumbled.

He wondered if she would read his thoughts; could she fathom that the quilt had been made by his first wife? It had been a piece of needlework of which she had been exceedingly proud. Justifiably so, it seemed, it had taken first prize at the county fair.

The farmer struggled with himself mentally. Should he tell his bride that his first wife had made the quilt and that it made him feel uneasy to see it lying there across the bed? Was it being disrespectful to use his dead wife's quilt to cover him and his new bride on their honeymoon night? Or should he heed his minister's advice and let the dead bury the dead?

His first wife *was* dead, he decided, crawling beneath the covers. He had made a promise to her that no fair-minded woman would expect him to keep.

But still he felt uneasy, and he could not stop thinking of his first wife as she lay dying and making him promise never to take another woman to his bed. Even as he reached for his new bride in order to consummate their marriage, the image of that dying woman seemed to lie there between them.

He was jolted back to the present by a woman's scream. He blinked his eyes, looked down in surprise at the woman who lay beneath him, screaming and pointing at something over his left shoulder.

He turned his head, and his heart nearly stopped beating. There, at the foot of the bed, was a shimmering image of a woman. It pointed an accusing finger at the couple in bed, then faded from sight.

As the frightened newlyweds lay in each other's arms, the only sensory impression that had managed to push itself through their fear was the fact that it was becoming inordinately hot beneath the covers. Their line of vision was finally distracted from the fading, ghostly figure by the thin tendrils of smoke that had begun to curl up from the quilt.

"The quilt is on fire!"

The farmer leaped out of bed and snatched the smoldering quilt. The moment it touched the plank flooring on their bedroom, the quilt burst into a brilliant ball of flame. Within seconds, nothing remained of his first wife's prize quilt but a few specks of soot and ashes. The jealous spirit of the farmer's first wife had apparently made certain that her quilt would cover no other occupant of her husband's bed.

Psychical researchers have long noted that the sexual adjustment to marriage can trigger such phenomena as uncontrolled manifestations of psychokinesis—the direct action of mind on matter. Combine sexual adjustment with conscious or unconscious feelings of guilt, and one may find the impetus for a psyche's bursting free of the body's inhibiting three-dimensional bonds. It may use virtually limitless mental talents, which may materialize other voices, other personalities, ghostly images, and the awesome power to, prismlike, focus enough energy to ignite fires.

Georgia B. from Cleveland, Ohio, had been married to Holden Fowler for only a few days when objects began to disappear and to reappear mysteriously. Fowler was several years older than his young wife, who was not yet out of her teens, and he admitted that he had been married once before. According to Fowler, his wife had died from blood poisoning after an operation. He was a private kind of person who valued his solitude; yet he had soon become lonely and had been eager to remarry.

One night Georgia awakened to find herself gasping for breath, an icy hand clutching at her throat. She grabbed the hand in desperation and tore it away.

"Are . . . you . . . try . . . trying to . . . strangle me?" she panted, shaking her husband awake.

It was apparent that the man was in a state of deep sleep. It had not been his hand at her throat. His eyes flickered open momentarily, and he mumbled, "It's in the black box," before he resumed his snoring.

"What's in the black box?" Georgia demanded, shaking him angrily. But he was oblivious both to the demands and her tiny hands thudding against his thick body.

Fowler, who had gained some reputation and considerable income as a brilliant, but eccentric, inventor, now set out to build his bride a new home. She, in turn, was eager to move, because she had concluded that the house must be haunted by some malignant entity intent upon strangling her.

On a number of other occasions, Georgia had awakened at night, gasping for breath, wrenching a cold, clutching hand away from her throat. After each attack, the only response that she could ever elicit from her soundly sleeping husband was, "*It's in the black box.*"

"When we moved into our new home," Georgia recalled, "my husband had the movers place an old trunk up in the attic. He said it had belonged to his former wife. I was busy and paid little attention to it. I was never a very curious woman. The trunk remained unopened for several years, and our new home was also blighted with horrible manifestations."

One night in the summer of 1968, as they sat reading in the living room, the couple was startled to hear a series of pitiful groans issuing from upstairs. Fowler grew suddenly pale, as if an invisible vampire-like phantom had instantly sucked out his blood.

"What on earth, or who on earth, is making such a dreadful noise?" Georgia asked her cowering husband. She begged him to go upstairs and investigate, but Fowler sat dead still, firmly a part of his easy chair. He gave no indication that he had heard his wife. He sat repeating over and over again: "It's in the black box! It's in the black box!"

Georgia decided that she had lived long enough with midnight stranglings, awful groans, and an eccentric husband. Her mother came to stay with her for a few days, and Georgia discussed her husband's bizarre behavior, the eerie manifestations that followed them from home to home, and her decision to obtain a divorce.

"I simply feel that I have lived with this situation long enough," she explained to her mother.

Her mother surprised her when she suggested that they go up to the attic and open the trunk that Holden Fowler had identified as having once belonged to his former wife.

Georgia was reluctant to pry into another woman's trunk, even if that other woman were dead, but her mother was determined that they might obtain some clue to the mystery among the belongings of Holden's former wife.

Georgia wrote:

We found that the trunk was not locked, and I opened the lid. We were greeted by the smell of musty clothes. Under the clothing

I found a black lacquered box. "Could this be the black box that your husband is always talking about in his sleep?" Mother asked.

I opened the box and found a small urn filled with ashes. "Her ashes!" Mother and I shouted at the same instant.

Georgia left her husband and later divorced him. She was convinced that the ashes in the crematory urn accounted for the thumps and moans that she had heard and for the cold hand that had tried to strangle her so many times in the night.

"Holden had never buried his first wife," she remarked. "It was her anger at him and her jealousy of me that made her want to kill me or drive me out of the house.

"Hers was a most angry, restless spirit. I never found out whether he ever buried her ashes, for I left him soon after my mother's visit."

According to Beryl H. of California, the spirit of a deceased lover appeared to her so that it might enjoy a last laugh at her expense.

"My first husband, Wendell J., was a real jealous sort of man, she wrote, "and it wasn't very long before I charged mental cruelty and divorced him. I was probably too young and flighty for marriage anyway, but I married again before I was twenty."

Beryl had not heard any news of Wendell for over a year, when one night, as she and her second husband lay in their upstairs bedroom, the image of Wendell appeared at the foot of their bed. Beryl remembered:

He just stood there looking down at us. I kept thinking of how jealous I had made him and how I had hurt him, and I was fearful at first that he had broken into our home to do us harm. But he just stood there looking at us, and then he started to laugh. He didn't say a single word, but he must have stood there laughing for nearly a minute. Then he turned and ran down the stairs.

Beryl and her husband were completely stunned, and several minutes passed before either of them could speak.

"What in hell was that?" her husband demanded, more of his

powers of reason than his equally startled wife.

"That . . . that was my first husband," she told him. "But how or why, I can't tell you."

Sleep was next to impossible for the remainder of the night, but the next morning at breakfast, Beryl found at least a partial answer to the mystery of the apparition in the daily newspaper. "We read that Wendell J. had passed away just a few moments before his spirit had appeared in our bedroom."

Beryl was still puzzled that the image of Wendell had been laughing. Such an apparition certainly did not fit into the stereotyped version of a mournful figure in a flowing white robe.

She did not have long to wait for an answer to her enigma, however. Her second husband confessed to her that he had been seeing another woman and that he had fallen in love with her. He asked to have his freedom. Beryl wrote:

> *It was now apparent to me why Wendell had materialized in our bedroom and had stood laughing over us. He was getting a good laugh at me. He had been terribly jealous of me, as jealous as I was toward my second husband, and I had left him, just as my second husband was about to leave me. There I was: married and divorced twice.*

A few years later Beryl married again, this time successfully. "Maybe Wendell destroyed my second marriage," she conjectured. "Maybe he decided that I should not find happiness until I had suffered at least one terrible heartbreak."

Dr. Loriene Chase, a clinical psychologist in Beverly Hills, California, writes a newspaper column dealing with psychological problems. One column was about a husband who complained that his wife was allowing her life to be controlled by the dictates of a Ouija board. To complicate matters, the wife insisted that her deceased former husband was the spirit who was communicating with her via the board.

According to the complaint, he had married the woman ten months after her first husband had died. His wife and her late husband had been happily married, and their union had produced three little girls.

One day the oldest girl came home with a Ouija board. When his wife tried her hand at the tripod, the message she spelled out

143

claimed to come from her deceased husband. The alleged spirit entity vowed that he still loved her and that he missed her. Soon the woman was weeping and talking to the board as if it were an embodiment of her first husband.

The woman's reliance upon the Ouija board progressed to the point where she had informed her second husband that they must obtain a divorce. She told him that she had known from the beginning that it had been a mistake for them to be married, for he was not at all like her first husband. According to the woman, her first husband catered to her whims and allowed her to run things the way she wished. Dr. Chase said in answer to the man's query:

> *It's possible that your wife feels a degree of guilt over marrying so soon after the death of her first husband or regrets the decision in some way. Add this to the fact that you are "different" and therefore unsatisfactory in your behavior toward her.*
>
> *If one or more of these factors are operative, it could be she has allowed these feelings to pyramid to the point where they have created the bizarre behavior you are now witnessing. The Ouija board would be her instrument as a way out of what she feels is a mistake.*

From the viewpoint of a clinical psychologist, perhaps the reports we examine in this chapter might be diagnosed as the manifestation of "a degree of guilt" that certain men and women have felt over marrying or courting others after the death of a mate or sweetheart. Indeed, unless one cynically wishes to conclude that all of the percipients of paranormal activity in this chapter are pathological liars, it seems that only two hypotheses can remain: (1) Conscious or unconscious feelings of guilt regarding infidelity toward a deceased mate or sweetheart have manifested themselves in bizarre and dramatic displays of psychic phenomena; or (2) the possessive, earthbound personalities of deceased men and women, confused by their sudden state of death, have remained to guard jealously their relationships with their surviving lovers.

There seems to be yet another category of spirits who return to haunt their former mates. These entities, if such they be, are much more benign, and they should rather be referred to as spirits who have maintained a somewhat proprietary interest in their Earth-plane love partners.

When her husband died in the fall of 1944, Dorothy Barnes of Vermont found herself beset with the many problems that a widow inherits upon the death of her mate. Since Dorothy had two children under four years of age, her most immediate problem was finding enough money to keep them all eating. Her husband had left only a minuscule estate, as far as his insurance policies went, but he had bequeathed her a section of timberland.

"A certain gentleman from the community made an offer that seemed fair to me," Dorothy said. "I knew that he had a reputation for pulling some rather slick deals, but I didn't think that he would try to take advantage of a young widow."

In his last days, as he had lay dying of cancer of the stomach, her husband had been unable to sleep at night. In those restless and painful hours, he would lie at Dorothy's side and gently stroke her hair. The night before Dorothy was to close the deal on the timberland, she lay in a light sleep, mentally debating the wisdom of her actions.

"I had not been sleeping long," she recalled, "when I became conscious of a hand stroking my hair. I knew that my husband was still watching over me, and I felt prepared to handle any situation."

Dorothy awakened, convinced that she should not sell the property. "I found out later that the timber alone was worth more than the price the man had offered me for the entire section of property."

The young widow struggled for over a year, trying to make ends meet. She was forced into the painful decision to board her children and temporarily set out alone to get a good job and to save money so that they could all be reunited as soon as possible. She found a young couple in a nearby city who had six or seven children already boarding with them and who seemed to be the ideal kind of temporary foster parents for her two children. Dorothy made all the necessary arrangements with the man and woman, and all that remained for her to do was to deliver her children early the next morning. Dorothy continued:

That night, as before, when I had been undecided about the sale of the land, I felt my husband's steady hand caressing my hair. I awoke knowing with the utmost certainty that I must not leave my children with that young couple. I knew that I must not go ahead with my plans to board them. Only a few weeks later, I read in the newspaper that the couple had been arrested for ill-treating the children in their care and for feeding them spoiled food.

After four years had passed since her husband's death, Dorothy found herself in a position wherein she was seriously considering remarriage.

It was no secret to me that Bob indulged in more than a social nip, but he seemed quite able to handle his drink. Oh, I had seen him drunk on more than one occasion, but I rationalized this by saying that everyone got a little tipsy once in a while.

She had nearly made up her mind to answer yes to Bob's entreaties, when, one night, she again felt the caress of her dead husband's hand. Dorothy changed her plans, reluctantly at first; then she experienced the knee-weakening sensation of a narrow escape when Bob's father called her to confess that Bob was an alcoholic and had already spent one expensive session of several months' duration in a hospital.

I later found out that the ever-vigilant spirit of my husband was not really jealous or possessive of me. For a time there, I thought that his presence would never allow me to marry, that his caressing hand would always come to find fault with any man who courted me, but such was not at all the case. I have now been happily married over thirty years. The beloved ghost of my first husband was looking after me only until he could safely leave me to fend for myself.

When Melissa W.'s husband died, she left the Midwest and moved to California, selling nearly everything she owned in the process.

For a little more than a year she was unable to obtain any kind of steady employment; then, finally, she found work as a laboratory technician in a small medical clinic. Four years later, one of the doctors, who had obtained a divorce from his second wife, asked Melissa to marry him.

She considered the man to be charming, but she had never felt entirely at ease with him. The longer they dated, the more Melissa doubted if she really loved him and if she should marry him. After a great deal of mental debate, Melissa at last accepted the doctor's proposal of marriage.

One night, shortly before their wedding date, Melissa, unable to get to sleep, sat up in bed reading. Then:

> *I noticed a strange radiation around the typewriter that I had left out on a desk across the room. I glanced about the room, trying to discover what could be casting such a peculiar glow on that particular spot. I tried to go back to my reading, but I found myself strangely attracted to that glowing globe of light. Then I heard the sound of typewriter keys being struck.*
>
> *I got out of bed and walked toward the desk. There, seated before the typewriter, his hands on the keys, was my late husband. I raised a hand as if to touch him; then both he and the strange illumination disappeared.*
>
> *I turned on the light, removed the sheet of paper from the typewriter. The spirit of my husband had typed these words: "Don't marry the doctor . . . he will cause you heartbreak, sorrow . . ."*

Confused, Melissa told her fiancé that she needed more time to think, and she asked that their wedding date be postponed. The doctor reluctantly agreed to her terms, although their relationship became somewhat strained.

Within a few months, the doctor killed himself in a fit of despondency over heavy gambling debts. Although he had somehow managed to keep it a secret from his colleagues in the clinic, the doctor had been a compulsive gambler.

The orthodox psychologist may assess Melissa's story as being the fantasy of a lonely woman who feared the reestablishment of an intimate relationship with a man; the psychic researcher may analyze the spirit writing of her husband as having been but Melissa's own automatic writing in which she unconsciously typed out her inner fears; but Melissa herself will always believe that her husband's love had survived the grave and had enabled him to return to warn her of an inadvisable union with another man.

9

SEXUAL MOLESTERS FROM SHADOWLAND
THE LOVE FORCE PERVERTED

A young woman from Oklahoma told one of my fellow psychical researchers that it is her habit to take a hot bath immediately upon returning from work, then loll about a few moments in the nude, usually reading on her bed. One night she lay on her stomach doing her nails, with her feet sticking out over the foot of the bed. She had lain there for several minutes when she felt someone grab her by the ankles and turn her over on her back. Then, she said:

> *Something invisible, yet of great strength, was seeking to spread my legs apart. I fought against this with all my will. The struggle must have gone on for several minutes. Every muscle in my thighs was screaming with pain of the constant tension, yet I would not yield and allow my genitals to be exposed in such a vulnerable manner.*
>
> *At last the pressure ceased, and I lay gasping on the bed. My nail polish had spilled, and the bedspread was stained. I had no time to worry about the mess, however. The foot of the mattress went down, as it does when a person sits on it. Still, I*

could see no one. The end of the bed went up again, and footsteps sounded walking to the head of the bed. My heart was thudding so hard in my chest that I could hardly breathe.

The footsteps stopped at the head of the bed, and I looked up to see the figure of a man standing there. His face looked like a zombie's, like someone who has been dead for a long time.

I couldn't make a sound, not even a squeak.

Then the hideous thing smiled and reached out a hand as if to touch me. It was changing its tactics. From attempted rape to a smile. It was grotesque, but there was something about its eyes that seemed to make me want to stop resisting it. At last I found my voice and screamed at it to get out of my room. Thank God it disappeared, and it has never returned.

In desperation, a thirty-nine-year-old widow in Pretoria, South Africa, appealed to the city council for new housing after repeated unwelcome advances from a spirit lover that had made her house its home.

Anna De La Ravera told newsmen that she and her children had noticed an eerie quality to the house shortly after they had moved in, in November of 1967. Mrs. De La Ravera said that she had found mysterious crosses chalked on the doors and a piece of pork on a nail in the master bedroom.

In March 1968, Mrs. De La Ravera returned home one day to find a man dressed in gray sitting on the front porch. "What do you want?" she demanded.

In response to her query, the man stood up and walked into the house through the closed and locked front door.

Although Mrs. De La Ravera could discover no trace of the phantom when she unlocked her door, he materialized that night in her bedroom and tried to pull the covers off her bed. The spirit wanted to make love, but Mrs. De La Ravera was having none of his persistent desires. According to the beleaguered widow, her unwelcome lover was covered with shaggy hair and had long, curved fingernails.

The passionate phantom relentlessly continued his amorous advances in the weeks that followed, until Mrs. De La Ravera could no longer tolerate another night in the accursed house.

"My two sons, aged nine and twelve, have seen nothing," she said in her appeal to the Pretoria City Council, "but my three-year-old daughter has cried, 'Mama, I'm scared. He'll bite me!'

"I have kept the lights on at night, but this does not seem to discourage the ghost. Once he switched off the lights and whispered to me, 'Be careful, I'm going to murder you!'"

The Pretoria City Council responded to the tormented widow's plight by assisting her in finding new housing. Once Mrs. De La Ravera had moved away from the diseased home that harbored the demanding sexual molester from the spirit world, she was able to spend her nights undisturbed by ethereal gropings.

The myths of the demon lover who ventures out on lusty forays in search of acquiescent human flesh is one that can be traced back to ancient times and whose strains can be found in all cultures. As the reader has just witnessed, such claims of supernatural sexual molesters cannot be relegated to a less sophisticated past. According to a good many men and women, who swear that they have encountered such sexual offenders from the spirit world, the demon lover is as much a bedroom nuisance in our supermarket-and-space-age culture as it was in the superstition-saturated and sexually tortured Middle Ages.

According to tradition, the *incubi* who pester women and the *succubi* who seduce men were born as a result of Adam's sexual relations with Lilith, a beautiful devil, often said to have been his first wife, or, in some versions, a "fantasy wife." If Lilith were but the personification of Adam's sensual imagination, then his intercourse with her would have been nothing more than masturbation.

In such an interpretation, the incubi and succubi would have been born of our first father's spilled seed and developed as children of a mortal father and his fantasized sex partner. Modern occultists theorize that the lusty human imagination, when excited by strong sexual daydreams and fantasies, ejaculates an ethereal sperm that provides the seed for succubi and incubi.

In the Middle Ages, theologians warned against masturbation on the grounds that waiting demons stood ready to transport the wasted semen for their own nefarious purposes. Nocturnal emissions were interpreted as the work of succubi, who excited sleeping males to the point of ejaculation.

The incubi and succubi played a dramatic role in the history of the Inquisition, as the reader might already have guessed. The

Tribunal must have listened with attitudes of disgust and fascination as a female witch told of the pain of having intercourse with her incubus and described his large, cold penis that brought a total chill to the flesh until it was well within her. Then, according to the witch, her belly would be set aflame. The male witches likewise described the vaginas as their succubi to be as ice.

The lusty incubi often seduced unsuspecting women by appearing to them in the guise of their husbands or lovers. To the male, the succubi usually manifested themselves as beautiful women.

As might be expected, the Christian hermits in their lonely desert hovels and the monks in their penitential cells were constantly harassed by sensuous succubi, who sought to tempt them into committing carnal sin. Likewise were certain nuns afflicted with persistent incubi, who tried to persuade them to break their vows of chastity. The epidemics of demon possession and erotomania, which swept such convents as those of Loudun, Louviers, Auxonne, and Aixen-Provence, have become classic cases of sexual hysteria.

In his book *Between Two Worlds*, Dr. Nandor Fodor tells of a modern struggle with an incubus that began for him on January 28, 1961, after he had appeared on a television program. A young woman contacted him by telephone and made an appointment to see him.

The young woman, whom he calls Jean, did not know until she arrived at his office that Fodor was a psychoanalyst. She knew only of his interest in the paranormal and his acceptance of things beyond the ken of the average man. She impressed Dr. Fodor with her plea that she needed help, and he became most interested in her highly unusual case.

Jean had been corresponding with a famous young man who had died shortly after his thirty-fourth birthday. On the day of "John's" death, Jean told Dr. Fodor that she had felt a presence in her bedroom and had the impression of a voice in her mind that said: "I am not dead."

Then there came pressures on her body, indentations on the bedspread from an invisible body, intimate caresses from unseen fingers. According to the young woman, she ". . . felt his manhood, accepted his lovemaking, and experienced an ecstasy from which 'wild horses would not drag me away.'"

After a few sessions of supernatural lovemaking, the full impact of the situation struck Jean and she sought to protect herself by prayer. When she first visited the psychoanalyst, she wore "an iron crucifix, wrapped in soft paper, over her vulnerable part. . . . It was a heavy crucifix, at least five to six inches long. . . . It was the crudest chastity belt that anyone could devise. . . ."

John, her demon lover, had begun to diagnose Jean's ills and prescribe drugs later found to be proper medications for such health problems. In addition, he hovered over her while she worked (Jean was a freelance writer) and sometimes supplied a word or two when she was undecided over proper phrasing.

Although such services might possibly be considered beneficial by those of a certain mental and emotional makeup, no woman could tolerate the possessive jealousy of a demon lover. John raised a psychic storm whenever Jean dated, and he would be all over her upon her return home.

Jean said that John had an odd odor, "a male sex odor," and she insisted that she could feel his body, "very light and exceedingly hot." The crucifix seemed to act as a deterrent against his sexual advances, but when she took a bath he would be there to rub his maleness into her.

Jean told her unseen lover that he was using her as a prostitute and she resented it. The ghost answered that he loved her.

"That does not make any difference," she had answered him. "You are in one world, I am in another!"

The young woman claimed that she had found many evidences that proved to her that her invisible lover was truly the surviving personality of the famous young man. John had written a number of autobiographical books before his death, and Jean was able to find several details about his earthly life that she could check in her conversations with the entity.

Jean did not tell her parents of her unearthly lover until after her first session with Dr. Fodor. The psychoanalyst convinced her that she would not be able to rid herself of the unwanted sexual advances of John's ghost unless she had the help of those who held her welfare most dear. Later, Jean's mother testified that she had seen the indentations that the ghost's body made on her daughter's bed, and on several occasions she had spent the night in Jean's room, attempting to keep the insatiable demon lover from sexually molesting the bedeviled girl.

Jean confessed to Dr. Fodor that she had not sought to deter John's ghost during their initial sessions of bizarre lovemaking. "I thought he was a good person and . . . would not harm me. After a while, however, I felt mesmerized. I began to fight him and he became violent. I was, by this time, repelled and disgusted. Now he is repugnant to me."

Jean had concluded that John had been a very different person from what the public had believed him to be. While alive, John had pretended to be a devout Catholic, but Jean claimed that he had even come to annoy her sexually while she sat in church.

Finally, through a series of attempted exorcisms on the part of spirit mediums, John became less of a nuisance and terror to Jean. In March of 1962, when Dr. Fodor last heard from her, he was at peace. The spirit still returned on occasion, but his visits were no longer sexually motivated.

Dr. Fodor concludes: "Whatever role her own love starvation may have played in the story, whatever latent psychic gifts grew on her physiological malfunctions, the reality of her tale of horror—shared by her whole household—cannot be doubted."

Could the incubi and succubi be born of the same sexual frustrations and difficulties in marital adjustment that incubate and hatch the noisy and destructive "bundle of projected repressions" we know as the rambunctious poltergeist?

The demon lover might be an inner-directed poltergeist—a psychokinetically projected personification of that dark, inaccessible part of the psyche in which resides the center of primitive instincts and the drive for sexual gratification. Perhaps a poltergeist becomes an incubus when its unconscious energy center has passed puberty and has either had preliminary sexual experience or else has thought a great deal about sex. The demon lover may cater to a particular psychic need brought about by the sexual frustration of the selfish, the self-centered, the narcissistic, who, because of their inner-directedness, fail to make a satisfactory sexual adjustment with a living love object and perhaps even prefer to fantasize a sex partner while masturbating.

Perhaps the ancients were right. Perhaps it is the spilled and misused seed that produces demons, demons born of misdirected sexual energy coupled with the frustrated creative drive of the subconscious. And maybe the occultists were also correct when they theorized that mental ejaculation of ethereal sperm fertilizes an as yet unnamed corner of man's psyche that has the ability to spawn "projected bundles of repressions."

I received a report some time ago about a "haunted house" that has within its walls a room wherein whoever has the courage to sleep on its canopied bed is beset with the most dreadful nightmares of suffocation and sexual assault. Screams have been heard echoing eerily down the corridors, and the evidence seems to indicate a point of emanation from somewhere within the psychically diseased room. According to tradition, a young woman was raped and murdered in that room, and the terrible emotion of that crime against her person has in some way penetrated the etheric atmosphere and almost attained a life of its own.

The skeptics say with finality that the evil thoughts and emotions of the living or the dead cannot overpower the healthy brain of a normal person. The mind cannot be subdued unless by physical distortion or disease.

There are intelligent men and women who feel otherwise. They are convinced that they have felt the touch of demons. In their experience, the admonition, "Get thee behind me, Satan," is by no means a fanciful directive.

Serious individuals claim to have undergone fearsome ordeals in which either they or their loved ones became the targets of vile entities that sought the possession of physical bodies and minds in order that they might enjoy the sensations of demonically aroused mortals who yield to ungodly temptations.

The skeptic will dismiss such stories as examples of psychological disorders, but certain psychical researchers and those who have been victimized argue that demonic possession is not insanity, for in most cases the possession is only temporary. The individual who has become possessed is unable to control himself, although he may be entirely conscious of the fiendish manipulation of his mind and body, and in many instances he may actually see grotesque and devilish faces before him.

HOW TO PROTECT YOURSELF FROM NEGATIVE ENTITIES

Frances has told me that I must be aware of the existence of lower-plane spirits who continually seek to possess the physical bodies of humankind. Although these entities seek always to control subjects whom they subjugate, the awareness that comes with spiritual enlightenment can render the spirits powerless.

Francie's guide, Kihief, has informed her that the Limbo spirits are not all-powerful. They cannot, for example, truly see the future. But they do have access to more precise probabilities than do mortals.

Most important, Frances emphasizes, the limbo spirits cannot achieve power over the human unless they are somehow invited into the person's private space—or unless they are attracted to an aura by that person's negative thoughts and actions.

The limbo spirits are parasites of the soul. They feed off negativity, and they are attracted to any human who emanates negative thoughts or who commits negative actions.

The limbo spirits crave to continue to experience the excesses of the flesh that they so enjoyed when they were in human bodies. For this reason, they are always seeking physical shells to possess in order to perpetuate their lusts.

Men and women are especially susceptible to such spirit invasion when they are exploiting one another sexually or when they have abused alcohol or drugs and their normal boundaries of control have been removed.

How can you best protect yourself from the limbo spirits of chaos? According to Frances, carefully observe the following ten "commandments":

1. Never enter meditation with the sole thought of obtaining personal satisfaction or ego aggrandisement. Selfish motivation may risk your becoming easily affected by those spirits who have become entrapped in a hellish domain of their own making, a limbo world of discordant vibrations.

2. Whenever you explore the psychic world through any of the occult arts, such as astrology, Tarot, Ouija boards, and so forth, practice a firm sort of mind control so that you will interact only with those entities in the realm of most loving and harmonious vibrations. Remember always to place the Golden Circle of Protection around you.

3. When seeking contact with higher intelligences, remember always that our physical reality is closer to the realm of the lower, more chaotic, frequencies, than it is to the dimension of the most

harmonious. Because we exist in a material world, the efforts of our psyches will always contain more of the lower vibratory realm than of the higher planes.

4. Prepare yourself for communication with an enlightened being from the higher spiritual worlds by bathing yourself in a wondrous expression of unconditional love. You will know no fear from such an encounter.

5. Know that should you meet a being from the chaotic realm, you will feel at once a prickling sensation that will seem to crawl over your entire body. You will instantly be filled with doubt. You will experience a mounting sense of terror or a distinct sensation of unease, depending upon the strength of the discordant vibrations emanating from the spirit.

6. If you should ever establish contact with a chaotic being, utter prayers and blessings of love at once. Fill your entire essence with unconditional love for all living things—including the manifesting or communicating spirit.

7. Understand that the realm of the limbo spirits houses all manner of discordant spirits. Be aware of the fact that the troubled spirits will continue their discordant ways beyond physical death, and they will often attempt to influence the minds, and thereby the lives, of those who will receive them. These spirits must be cast out from your mind and your life.

8. Keep always in your mind that if you wish to prevent contact with the entrapped entities of limbo, you must practice loving all living things unconditionally; and you must seek to elevate the consciousness of all humankind by your thoughts, words, and deeds.

When you vibrate with the highest form of love, when your purpose is that of the angels, you will be able to make contact with those entities who exist in the realm of the highest vibrations. You will not have to fear encountering the angry spirits of limbo, for you will only receive meaningful, inspirational contact with the angelic beings from the realm of the highest order.

9. Realize that evil or negativity is an imbalance, a chaotic, ignorant, mindless energy or vibration. It is a destructive energy, the opposite of growth and productivity.

The energy of negativity operates at an abnormal rate and becomes an insane, frenzied energy, capable of much destruction. When you are negative, depressed, and do not vibrate with unconditional love, you place yourself "on target," right in the path of that chaotic, mindless, destructive vibration that comes from the world of the lesser energies, the lower frequencies.

10. Never forget that all that exists vibrates at its own particular frequency, at its own energy level. You can develop the power and the ability to raise or lower your vibrational frequency. This choice is what distinguishes us from the animals.

TRANSFORMING NEGATIVITY

If you should sense the presence of negative entities in your environment, practice this exercise:

Bend your elbows and lift your hands, palms outward to the level of your chest. Take a comfortably deep breath, then emit the universal sound of "OM" in a long drawn-out chant: O-O-O-O-M-M-M.

Repeat this until you are able to feel the energy tingling the palms of your hands. This is a good exercise for raising both your vibrations and your spiritual strength.

Once you feel more positive, bring your palms toward one another until you are able to feel the Love Force or the Life Energy as a palpable "substance" between them. Focus upon this energy.

Visualize the energy moving upward from your palms to your fingers. Feel it moving up your arms, your shoulders, your neck, your face. Image the energy feeding new life, new "blood" to your entire physical being.

Utter the universal sound of "OM" once again. Visualize the energy moving up to the crown chakra, then cascading down in sparks of golden light, as if you were being enveloped by the downward pouring of a roman candle. Impress upon your consciousness that those "sparks" represent new, positive energy that is descending around your physical body and forming a vital *protective shield* against discordant and negative entities.

TRANSFORMING NEGATIVITY THROUGH THE LOVE FORCE

Suppose you feel threatened with negativity by a vicious person or by an unseen presence that has left you feeling frightened and very much alone in the world. Perhaps you are away from home, and you feel that chaotic forces in that strange environment have been activated against you.

Go to a place where you can be alone to reestablish your emotional and spiritual equilibrium. Sit quietly for a moment. If possible, play some soft, restful music. It is always a good idea to travel with your cassette player and a number of New Age music albums in your suitcase.

After you have begun to calm yourself, say, as you inhale, *"I am."* On the outbreath, say, *"relaxed."*

Repeat this process a number of times. Take comfortably deep breaths.

"I am," asserts your sovereignty and your individual reality on the intake. *"Relaxed"* positively affirms your calm condition on the outtake.

Now visualize someone you love who is extremely positive and who shares your philosophy, your perspective, your point of view about life and the cosmos. This may be a spouse, a friend, a lover, a child.

See the person on whom you are focusing your visualization turn toward you with a smile of love. See the person extending his or her hand to yours. Feel the touch of fingertip to fingertip. Sense the electrical crackle of energy moving between you. Experience the warmth of the Love Force that flows between you.

Visualize your taking that person's hand in your own. Feel comforted knowing that there is one who loves you and who exhibits concern for you.

See this shared love erecting a barrier between you and the negative bombardment to which you are being subjected.

Next image you or your loved one reaching forth a hand to take another's. Visualize yet another loving man or woman who is being welcomed to your circle. See that person joining you, smiling as he or she takes a place beside you to add to your fortress of bonded love energy.

Continue to visualize other men and women joining your circle of love until you have built as large a barrier as you feel that you need to face the hostility or the negativity that is being directed against you by seen or unseen entities. Feel strength, born of love, swell within your breast.

Visualize the Love Force moving from member to member of your magic circle. See the Golden Light of Protection encircling your group externally. See the energy of unconditional love flowing from one to another as you visualize yourself holding hands and linking your vibratory frequencies.

After you have seen and felt the energy moving among your circle, visualize the ultraviolet light of the Love Force descending from above and touching each of your members on the crown chakra. Feel yourself vibrating with the greatest emanation of love from the very heart of the universe.

Hold this image and this energy as long as it is needed.

When you have become completely fortified and calmed, it would be best to go to bed and enjoy a peaceful night's rest. If this is impossible and you must return to encounter the negativity, know that you will do so totally prepared and reinforced for any situation that might arise. Stride confidently into the "arena," knowing that you are linked together in an unbreakable bond of love with those kindred souls who have joined you in the Love Force.

10
MULTIDIMENSIONAL BEINGS OF LOVE AND LIGHT

~~~

Gina and Julie Oltersdorf believe firmly that the benevolent stranger who paid them a visit when they were young girls in the Midwest was an angel.

> *It was in December of 1944, Gina remembered. We were living in an old farmhouse that seemed to have more cracks than Daddy could patch with the bits of tarpaper that he managed to scrounge from his boss. We had lost the farm the year before, and we lost Momma to typhoid fever that summer.*
>
> *There were the four of us kids—Steve and Karl, besides us two girls—who had to nestle next to the old oil burner in the front room and try to keep warm enough to do our homework at night.*
>
> *It was just before Christmas that Julie came down with a really bad fever. We had but one blanket apiece, but we all tried to pile the covers on Julie when we were doing our chores and our homework. Normally, we walked around that old farmhouse*

you have undoubtedly seen examples of his fine craftsmanship. Although he had been a freelancer for many years, Harry decided to take a job as a staff artist with a leading national publication in New York. Just after he had completed placing all of his financial eggs in one basket, Harry was summarily fired.

It was two in the afternoon. Somehow he had to face the hard reality of becoming suddenly unemployed when both he and his wife had just grown accustomed to receiving a weekly paycheck. And, yes, somehow he had to tell his *wife* what had happened! Would it be possible to make their meager savings hold out long enough for him to reestablish his former connections and solicit freelance work once again?

Although it was not at all his custom to do so, Harry wandered into a bar and ordered a stiff drink. He had been walking the streets in a rather disoriented state, and he paused for a moment to try to get a fix on precisely where he might be. The address on the paper napkin under his drink told him the location of the bar he had randomly chosen, but he knew that he had never before seen the inside of the place.

"May I join you, Harry?" asked a pleasantly smiling stranger, his hand already resting on the back of a chair at Harry's table.

"Why not," Harry mumbled. Then, after a moment's scrutiny, he asked: "How did you know my name?"

"Oh, I know a lot about you, Harry," the man said. "It's tough being fired, but you must not become discouraged."

Harry squinted over the edge of his glass. Was the stranger a staff member of the magazine whom he had not yet met? After all, he had barely been there long enough to become adjusted to the working hours, to say nothing of meeting all of the staff members.

The man smiled and denied working on the magazine but he proceeded to tell Harry just how much he really knew about the most intimate details of his life.

Harry said:

> *I was stunned. This guy was the most incredible psychic I have ever met. Not only had I never seen him before and he had called me by name, but he seemed to know everything about me. He knew my birthdate, my wife's and kid's birthdates. He knew all about my work and how I had just been fired. After a few minutes, I just sat there and listened to him with my mouth hanging open.*

Then, the most amazing thing of all—He told me where to go for a job. He told me the address and who to see. And he gave me a little sermon about keeping my chin up and never becoming discouraged—you know, about how we never really walk alone in life. There's always someone to reach out a helping hand.

Harry was so heartened by the man's message and the tip on the new job that it took him a moment to realize that the stranger was no longer speaking to him. He turned to see him walking out the front door.

"The funny thing was that I ran after him to thank him," Harry said, "but he must have blended right in with the people on the street, 'cause he was nowhere in sight. I was right behind him, too, but I lost him."

Before he called his wife with the bad news, Harry went directly to the publication that the stranger had recommended. He asked for the editor the man had suggested, and within another hour he was hired to begin illustrating the issue in current deadline. Harry has often remarked:

"I wish that I knew that psychic's name. I went back to the bar many times, thinking that he might frequent the place, but I never saw him again. I tried to describe him to the bartenders who work there, but none of them claimed to recognize him at all. I'd like to thank that guy. He was the world's greatest psychic!"

Was the stranger a psychic, I have asked Harry, or was he a multidimensional missionary, an angel?

Could any man, no matter how psychically sensitive he might be, have known such an incredible amount of information about any other human being?

Or was the stranger a *nonhuman* being with insights, knowledge, and information far beyond any mortal's ability to deduce or to prognosticate?

A man who had once served with the U.S. Rangers, an elite, crack corps of rugged fighting men organized during the early days of World War II, told me a remarkable story that he swore was true. Since Mac was known as a businessman of high integrity it would seem that he would have little reason to muddy the facts surrounding the circumstances that saved his life.

Mac got separated from his men after a vicious encounter with some brutally efficient members of General Rommel's Afrika Korps. Battered, and a bit the worse for wear, Mac tried to go sparingly on the little water he had left in his canteen. But the merciless inferno of the desert seemed to be scorching every drop of moisture from his body.

He knew that he was dehydrating quickly, and he did his best to conserve his energy. At the same time, Mac realized that to remain stationary was no guarantee of survival.

When Mac was finally found several days later, his rescuers brought in a man mightily in need of hospital care, but a man very much alive and not at all dehydrated. In fact, his canteen was more than half full.

How had Mac survived? Although he is essentially an unchurched man, whose father was an avowed atheist, Mac asked to tell his story to a priest, Father Tony.

"An angel brought me water in the desert," Mac told the astonished clergyman. Mac had somehow managed to keep his canteen with him, and he handed it to the priest, sloshing the water around as he did.

Hearing such testimony from a tough, no-nonsense soldier intrigued Father Tony to the extent that he asked to have the water analyzed. Later, he told Mac that the chemists had said the water was extremely pure, containing none of the minerals or other substances that would be indigenous to that area of the desert.

Father Tony was tempted to call it holy water.

BEINGS OF LOVE AND LIGHT

According to a recent Gallup Poll, three in ten respondents stated that they had experienced a moving religious experience and "otherworldly feelings of union with divine beings." Sex, education, or age of the respondents did not make a significant difference.

Dr. Elisabeth Kubler-Ross, the eminent doctor who has revolutionized our view of death and dying, told a hushed audience of several hundred psychologists, psychiatrists, and mental health experts attending a medical conference in San Diego that she had been visited the night before by three "spirit creatures" who had instructed her to tell the assembled doctors about the reality of "spirits."

Dr. John Lilly, the pioneering neurophysicist, biologist, psychoanalyst, and distinguished explorer of inner space, relates his encounters with his spirit guides in his famous work *The Center of the Cyclone*.

Ever since she was a child of five, my wife Frances has insisted that the angel who appeared to her was not the product of a dream or imagination.

Today, Frances is a holistic teacher of international reputation, who conducts workshops for medical doctors, psychiatrists, nurses, and teachers. She still asserts the appearance of the angel was an actual event in her life and that the experience was real and true. And she consistently demonstrates that a steady interaction with angelic intelligences has been a continuing factor in her life from that day to the present.

In tests conducted in 1978 and 1979, science's most sophisticated new instrument for assessing the truth of anyone's claims, the Psychological Stress Evaluator (PSE), proved the validity of Frances' angelic visitation and the subsequent information that has been relayed to her.

In her thought-provoking, inspirational book, *Reflections From An Angel's Eye*, Frances tells how an angelic spokesman, together with four auxiliary beings, came down through the ceiling of her parents' bedroom, where she was seated on the edge of the bed beside an open window, watching her father hang a picture. Her father was placed into a state of suspended animation while the principal angel, whom she later came to know as Kihief, presented her with certain instructions.

He alighted so gently that he stood almost directly before me, and I wasn't certain if he ever touched the floor.

His white robe was draped over one shoulder, and the wind made it flow in and out around his body. His hair was straw-colored and straight ... coming down to the base of his neck. His eyes were light, wide-set; he had a large, full jaw and fair skin.

He began to speak, rising and falling in tone, as one would sing and talk at the same time in a falsetto voice. I remembered several phrases for years, though some of them made little sense to me at the time.

One phrase he sang-talked to me was, "Like unto another Christ child you will be." I have assumed that there is some underlying symbolism to that statement. Please believe me, I have no great aspirations toward martyrdom. And I know that there may exist many others with a similar mission to operate on the Christ vibration or consciousness.

Forrest L. Erickson, one of the nation's foremost PSE examiners, was the expert who evaluated Frances' test. His findings prove that in every instance tested Frances was totally innocent of deception. Her voice was free of any stress that would indicate an untruthfulness.

The PSE detects, measures, and graphically displays guilt-revealing variations in the human voice. The PSE machine records the subject's voice patterns and indicates certain stress-related tremors that are controlled by the involuntary muscles triggered by the subconscious mind.

The PSE is used by criminologists, law enforcement officers, lawyers, doctors, insurance company investigators, fire officials, and psychiatrists. Several courts in the United States accept PSE findings as admissible evidence in court and judge the machine a reliable instrument in proving innocence.

Included in Erickson's evaluation of Francie's test are the following assessments:

"The angel was coming down through the ceiling."
Evaluation: "True."
"Like unto another Christ child you will be."
Evaluation: "True. This is very true."
"I have felt continual interaction with these beings."
Evaluation: "True."
"I am taken out of the body and shown visions."
Evaluation: "That appears true."

Fran's description of the angelic entities as being taller than humankind, very muscular, and physically attractive was evaluated in the following way: "Some doubt expressed that they were taller. [Remember, Francie was only five when the experience occurred.] It is true that they were muscular in appearance and not thin at all. Essentially, all her statements appear true."

For centuries, our prophets, mystics, and revelators from all cultures and religious persuasions have attested that they have interacted with angelic intelligences. Now it would appear that our most sophisticated truth-detecting instrumentation has proved the reality of angelic contact by declaring that a sincere revelator has been truthful in her account of the momentous event.

CONTACTING MULTIDIMENSIONAL BEINGS

Frances always instructs her students that the first step in preparing for the meditation that will bring contact with angelic entities is to erase anger and hatred from one's being and to fill oneself with unconditional love for all living things.

If this seems an impossible task, think pity and compassion for those for whom you feel hatred. Pity them for their lack of knowing.

Next, cleanliness within and without is important.

Begin with the total cleansing of your body, and the desire to be clean within will follow.

Frances has found that a vegetarian diet best prepares her for blending with the higher vibrations. She does not believe that one should partake in the death and the suffering of one's fellow creatures on Earth.

We are to feel and to "know" conditional love and to fill ourselves with unconditional love for *all* living things before we are ready to receive and to do that which we were born to do.

When one seeks contact with multidimensional beings, he or she must be prepared to become far more aware than previously deemed possible.

Proper prayer is the next step, Frances states.

Begin with a prayer of love, asking for guidance in everyday life and with a request for protection from the chaotic vibrations that exist as a result of the polarization of the Highest Vibration of Order, a state that first came into existence a long time ago. Pray and feel the enveloping warmth of love and protection that surrounds you.

The last step is the *inner* cleansing.

Picture before you a crystal river of sacred, healing water that pours forth from the heavens. This is special water—energy-water.

Visualize yourself walking to the river and dipping down into the water. It is only as deep as the height of your heart. Wash off all negativity, all guilts, all pains, all past sufferings, all debilitating memories. See yourself washing yourself until you are as clean as a new-born babe.

Dip down and bathe your chest area, your shoulders, and your back, in particular.

Know that this healing, holy water cleanses *within* as well as *without*.

Now walk to the opposite shore of the river, fresh, clean, renewed.

See yourself walking a grassy knoll. See upon its top a golden, bejeweled chalice, filled with a milky-white substance—unconditional love from God.

Drink that fluid, and visualize yourself as a spiritual tea kettle, complete with spout where your heart is. Picture yourself pouring unconditional love on all living things.

See before you a lovely crystal city. Open the large golden door to the city. Enter the door and meet the angelic beings who wait to teach you love, wisdom, and knowledge.

Visualize and perform these important steps nightly, and they will become a reality, Frances advises all those who seek inner awareness.

Many props can aid you in achieving the required state of relaxation. Try background music; flickering, revolving lights; luminous stars that glow from your ceiling; etc. These stimuli will intensify your belief construct and aid you in projecting yourself to the other domain.

Frances emphasizes that in the initial stages it is very important to focus your conscious mind on an object for a period of time so that you can successfully separate the conscious from the subconscious and learn control of the latter.

You must learn to put your physical body to sleep while awakening your spiritual self.

Each time the preparatory steps are followed and the more they are believed, shorter will be the concentration—and heavier will be the realization.

If necessary, one can select an object for concentration, such as an imagined dot between the eyes, a portrait of a holy figure, an appointed area on the wall, a blank screen.

Any thought that enters your mind should be *gently* removed; never *shove* the intruding thought away. Tell it that you will think of it later, then gently remove it from your mind.

With continued practice, any sincere student may learn to establish an awareness of other dimensions, Frances promises.

Soon you will be able to thought-travel. Thought-traveling is the means by which you will truly reach the dimension where the angelic beings dwell.

Some see themselves crossing a bridge before they enter the angelic domain, Frances says. Others speak of a golden temple wherein they are given special teachings.

Many tell of a booming voice that enquires: "Are you ready?"

If you hear that voice, say yes, and you will make contact with angelic beings and spiritual travelers just as Frances has done.

A PRODUCTIVE PRAYER FOR PROTECTION FROM NEGATIVE ENTITIES

Beloved _____ [Say the name of your guide if you are aware of it; if not, say "Light Being."] establish your protective light energies around me.

Erect a shield of love about me that is invincible, all-powerful, and impenetrable.

Keep me absolutely protected from all things that are not of the Light.

Keep me immune from all imperfect vibratory rates.

A REQUEST FOR REJUVENATION

When you are feeling at a low energy level and need instant strength, ask in this manner:

Beloved _____, *charge* me with your great strength.

Charge me with your light and your love.

Charge me as if I were a battery, totally susceptible to your energy.

Charge each of my vital body functions with strength and energy.

Keep me ever sensitive to your guidance and your direction.

THE VIOLET LIGHT
OF TRANSFORMATION

The Violet Light from the Source constitutes the highest vibratory level.

There are moments on the Earth plane when we clumsily and thoughtlessly transgress against others. Summoning the violet light of the Love Force assists you in balancing your account. It can help you to *transform* the negativity that you may have sown.

Certain masters have likened the violet light to an eraser. When you learn to use it often and opportunely, you may erase all from your vibrations that are not of the Light and of Love.

Other teachers have said that the violet light may be used to dissolve disease, to alleviate suffering, to cure illness.

Disease, suffering, and illness are, after all, manifestations of chaos and discord. Suffusing them with the violet light of love may alter them and raise their vibratory levels to points of transformation.

A DAILY RITUAL
OF TRANSFORMATION

You may wish to use the violet light in a daily ritual of transformation.

Call for the violet light and ask that your angelic guide connect you to the Love Force. Visualize the violet light moving over you in a wave of warmth. See it touching every part of your body. Feel it interacting with each cell.

Say inwardly or aloud to your guide:

Beloved _____, assist me in calling upon the highest of energies and the Source of All That Is. Activate the Love Force within me so that I may channel directly to the Oneness.

Provoke the law of harmony for myself and for all those of us of mortal clay who stray from the Light.

Permit the violet light to move around and through me. Allow the transforming energy to purify and to elevate all impure desires, incorrect concepts, anger, wrongdoings, and improper memories.

Keep this light bright within me.

Replace all chaotic vibrations around me and *in* me with pure energy, the power of Love, and the fulfillment of the Divine Plan.

AN AFFIRMATION UPON ARISING

An affirmation that you might wish to utter each morning upon arising could be stated in this way:

Beloved _____, I feel you on this new day activating the Love Force within me and charging me with perfect health, joy, illumination, wisdom, and the fulfillment of those physical things that I truly do need for my good and gaining.

CO-CREATING WITH THE LIGHT BEINGS

Remember always that each individual is a creator. What you *think*, you *create* on some level of consciousness, on some vibratory plane.

Where your attention is, there you are.

What you wish, you will become.

What you meditate upon, you will be.

Therefore, if you give attention to your guide and the Love Force for even one minute a day, you will receive much positive energy and bring much good into your life.

If for just one minute each day, you think of your guide and feel the Love Force moving into your body . . . just sixty seconds visualizing the most powerful energy in the universe moving into your fleshly shell . . . just a tiny portion of your daily schedule to fix your attention upon the harmonizing of your fleshly vehicle . . . just one minute to turn on your inner "light switch," you, with the direction of your guide, can become master of your reality!

THE IMPORTANCE OF HUMILITY

Be mindful that you always remain humble in the presence of your guide. Constantly remind your arrogant ego and your rational intellect that the Love Force is responsible for the significant actions of your life.

To be humble, however, does not mean that one must be easily compromised with material plane wrongs and the weaknesses of the human condition. I refer only to humility in the presence of higher intelligences.

SOME WORDS OF ADVICE

After you have established contact with your guide, you will discover that what you formerly termed "premonitions" may be promptings from higher intelligence.

Important: When you receive a premonition that warns you against a particular course of action or of an act of negativity that may come to you, you must understand that the act of *receiving* a premonition does not mean that the adverse situation *must* take place. Interpret such a premonition as the mechanism of your guide bringing the matter to your attention so that you may apply the violet light and transform the situation, thereby avoiding its unfavorable action.

Important: In the application of each of these exercises of contacting the guide *understand completely* that the true application of these energies requires more than the mere recitation of words. You must *feel* the correctness and the importance of what you are doing.

A Warning: Some teachers have stated that an insincere or ineffective recitation of such exercises could accumulate into thought forms, which, one day, will require transformation. How unfortunate it would be to have to dissipate thought-forms of one's own creation that have simply puddled into vortexes of chaotic, misdirected energy.

Do not permit yourself to cry out to your guide for assistance when you and your inner resources could handle the problem with a bit of effort.

Do not allow yourself to become spiritually lazy. Do not call upon your guide to assist you with every rock and chuckhole on your life path.

Remember always that you came into your fleshly shell in order to experience growth and gaining. The Father-Mother-Creator does help those who help themselves.

Consider your guide to be a helping hand that is to be grasped only when you *really need* to boost upward to solve a truly difficult situation.

11

WE HAVE LOVED BEFORE

"Simon . . . Simon de Montfort, the pig! I hate him! We will never surrender!"

Frances and I glanced at each other in open astonishment. It was happening again. Seven hundred years ago, Pope Innocent III had appointed de Montfort, an accomplished military leader, to the task of conducting a crusade against the Albigensians, cultured men and women of southern France who had been declared "enemies of the Church." A true soldier, de Montfort had warmed to the task. Although it took him twenty years of warfare against the beleagured Albigenses, he at last managed to exterminate 100,000 men, women, and children.

But now, lying there before us in an entranced state, we were listening to a young woman from Texas voicing the echoes of that terrible time of bloodshed and carnage. She had come to us in the hope of finding an origin for a series of troubled dreams of fleeing to caves in a mountainous region. What we were now hearing was an eyewitness account of the fall of Beziers in 1209. She had joined the increasingly large numbers of men and women we have discovered who, while in an altered state of consciousness, relived a past-life experience as a member of the Albigensian sect.

Surprised as we were, we could not help marveling at the phenomenon of the "Albigensian Connection," for it would seem that so many of us who experienced that horror were, in one way or another, coming together again.

Yes, I said, "us," for Fran and I had an instant and spontaneous recall upon our first meeting that we had shared that past-life experience together. In fact, although there are obviously many reasons why we have come together again, it may well have been that recall of the Albigensian life experience that cemented our essential selves into a once and future incarnation.

As I wrote in *The Seed*:

> *Ever since I was a young boy I have had fleeting images of having been a Spanish knight. In one of the most memorable scenes, I remember sitting astride my horse, observing a picturesque cottage in the woods. Screams alert me to behold a blonde girl in a peasant blouse and dark skirt running to escape a great, bearded lout, who is chasing her on horseback. I intervene and slay the brutish man.*
>
> *When Francie and I met, we had an instantaneous Soul recognition on several levels. Then, incredibly, I found myself saying, "You were the blonde girl in the forest."*
>
> *Francie blinked back her astonishment, then smiled and nodded. "And you were the knight who saved me."*
>
> *Remarkably, numerous psychic sensitives have recalled the scene quite independently of one another. In widely separated sections of the country, psychically talented men and women have told us how "Brad was a knight who saved Francie from a big, bearded brute of a man."*

As we came together as man and woman, so did a more complete past-life attunement arrange the fragments of memory into a more coherent story.

The scene was in the Pyrenees mountain region. We were members of the Albigensian sect living in Beziers when Pope Innocent III launched a crusade against the city more than 700 years ago.

Frances was a seeress who lived in a cottage in the forest. I was a Spanish nobleman who had spoken out against the Holy Roman Church and had fled across the Pyrenees to join the Albigensians.

In that lifetime, Fran's Soul embodiment was a channel for Higher Intelligences, just as she is today. She was in constant communication with an angel, who guided her then, as he does in her present Soul experience.

"Don Ricardo" saved "Francesca," the lovely witch of the woods, from a brutal attack by a knight who had forsaken his vows of chastity. The two became inseparable from that moment to their deaths—his, defending the walls of Beziers against the Pope's armies; hers, by execution when the walls fell.

In recent years we have amassed increasing amounts of evidence that hundreds of those entities who were put to sword and torch in 1209 are returning on the great spiral of rebirth to bring their consciousness into new-age awareness. In conference after conference, in seminar after seminar, we meet those men and women who declare their memories of having been members of the Albigensian sect.

According to scholars, the Albigenses' real offense, their "heresy," was their opposition to the sacramental materialism of the Medieval Church. The cultural life of the Albigenses far outshone that of any other locality in Europe. In manners, morals, and learning objective historians state that the Albigenses deserved respect ". . . to an infinitely greater extent than the orthodox bishops and clergy . . . It is now conceded that the court of Toulouse was the center of a higher type of civilization than existed elsewhere in Europe."

Most experts on this historical period agree that the twenty years of warfare against the Albigenses ruined the most civilized nation in thirteenth-century Europe. The pitiless cruelty and brutal licentiousness, which was habitual among the Crusaders, achieved new depths of inhumanity against the Albigenses. No man was spared in their wrath. No woman was spared in their lust. It has been observed that no Roman, Hunnish, Muslim, or Mongol conquerer ever wiped out a Christian community with greater savagery.

Because the testimony of what the Albigensians believed was wrung out under extreme torture from those who survived the massacre, it has been very difficult to understand their true belief structure until very recent times. Research now indicates that far from the devil-worshipping monsters that warranted extermination, the Albigenses were devout, chaste, Christian humanists, who loathed the excesses of the Medieval Church. They were metaphysicians, spiritual alchemists, herbalists, healers, and societal helpers—all with a very practical turn of mind.

We find similar expressions of their belief structure in the *Gnostic Gospels*, in the Essenes at Qumran, in the Egyptian Mystery Schools. Most readers with metaphysical interests would feel very much at home in the Albigensian communities of southern France. A true time machine can exist between the New-Age consciousness and the communities that received Papal condemnation 700 years ago.

Since most of the Albigensian communities were first sacked, then burned, their records and their libraries were destroyed. Perhaps the only accounts of these forgotten people lie in the Soul memories of men and women living today. And whether one believes in Akashic Records, reincarnation, genetic memory, or the collective unconscious, it may be that such an affront to the human spirit can never be obliterated. Fragments of Soul may be crying out to remind the world that goodness can never be truly destroyed—even in the name of orthodoxy.

BORN AGAIN THROUGH THE LOVE FORCE

There are, perhaps, no tales quite as romantic as those of reincarnated lovers who have once again managed to find each other over the span of centuries.

Many men and women have told Frances and me of having entered happy marriages as a result of a conviction that they had been sweethearts, lovers, or spouses in a past life. To attain this goal of reunion, some of the reborn lovers have undergone a great deal, including divorces, separation from their children, and the animosity of friends and relatives.

Certain individuals have entered man-woman relationships—marital or otherwise—consciously unaware of their previous life ties and their karmic debts to one another. These love partners may experience personal anguish and find that their lives have become miserably complicated.

From all over the United States they have come to us—men and women with marital maladjustments, emotional entanglements, and sexual traumas. Through a unique method of counseling, combined with hypnotic regression, we have discovered that the origins of many of these difficulties lie in previous lifetimes. We have become convinced that not only have we lived before, we have loved before.

Whether such reincarnational recalls are fantasies or actual past lives coming forth as memories, many men and women have obtained definite and profound release of present life phobias by reliving the origin of the trauma in some alleged former existence. A belief in the theory of reincarnation is not necessary for the subject to experience a benefit from the cathartic vision or fantasy.

Psychologists have long realized that discovering the cause of an existing condition releases the effect of its hold on the subject. By reliving an alleged past life, a subject is able to release fully his emotions and is able to accept responsibility for an action which he now considers already performed and done with in a previous lifetime. Once the subject has made the transfer of responsibility to the present life and has recognized that the "fault" lies in a time far removed from current concerns, he is able to deal with the matter without shame.

While in consultation with us, the subjects relive their past life experiences and describe them in great detail. They name countries, cities, years; they provide information about the current events of the day, the state of the weather, the manner of dress in vogue.

Here, from the hundreds in our files, are several capsule case studies. I have selected these stories because Fran and I feel that they effectively demonstrate the thesis that we have lived and loved before. In addition, we have found that in sharing such accounts as these with our lecture and seminar audiences, many men and women have found themselves identifying with the situations, receiving great inspiration from their resolutions, and gaining insight into their own problems.

When Esther came to us, she was suffering from a general insecurity about her marriage with Carl. She felt that her husband was sometimes aloof, complete in himself without her.

Through counseling and regression, we learned that the two had shared a past life in New Bedford, *circa* 1850. Esther had fallen in love with Carl, a young seafaring man. Although he was amorous enough when he was home, he always answered the call of the sea and left Esther waiting on the dock. Their present marriage became more secure when Esther was helped to realize that, in this lifetime, Carl had come home to her arms to stay.

From the first moment of their initial meeting, Dick and Marta could hardly keep their hands off each other. Their strong attraction was complicated by Dick's marriage to Ann. Through regression, we learned that Dick and Marta had shared a life together in ancient Egypt.

Marta had been of royal lineage, and Dick had been a military officer who lusted mightily after the woman he was assigned to protect. Indignant that the temporal status of birth kept them separated, Dick made his feelings known to his high-born lady. Marta reciprocated his affections, but the reward for their affair had been assassins' arrows for Dick and poison for Marta. Now, after Dick's divorce, they are together after nearly 3000 years and happily making up for lost time!

Millie had large, dark circles under her eyes as she sobbed out her story. She was considering divorce because Clark was obsessed with his work to the point of almost total neglect of their children. He was a workaholic who begrudgingly took time off only for holidays and birthday observances.

Through a deep session of consultation, Millie relived a life of terrible poverty and famine in which she had also been married to Clark. In anguish, she saw them burying five of their eight children, as one by one they starved to death. Once again she heard Clark's tormented self-condemnation as he cursed himself for being a poor provider.

She returned to her marriage suffused with greater understanding of Clark's obsession and with a plan of how she might alleviate the sense of guilt he carried with him from a previous lifetime.

Mark could hardly look us in the eye when he came to us. He did not wish to hurt his wife Carol, but from time to time he became so enraged at her for the smallest of marital infractions that he beat her severely. The two were in their early twenties, too young to be mired in such tragic domestic circumstances.

Through regression, we learned that Mark recalled a life as a Jewish victim of the Nazi concentration camps. In that existence, Carol had been a sadist who had taken great delight in torturing prisoners and in collecting hideous trophies from their mutilated bodies. She had been particularly vicious to Mark, and with his dying breath, he had vowed to make her pay for her brutalities. It required a number of sessions to help them restructure their lives in a positive expression of the remarkable karma that had reunited victim and murderer.

We could understand Bart's frustration when he brought his attractive wife Kim to us for consultation. Tearfully, Kim admitted that even though she loved her husband she simply could not enjoy sex with him.

After an in-depth consultation, it was discovered that the two had been previously united in a primitive relationship in the Middle East. Bart had had several wives and had treated them all like baby factories. He was interested only in adding to his prestige and wealth by fathering sons to tend his flocks. He had impregnated Kim nine times in that prior life experience, and he had murdered three girl babies before her anguished eyes.

The karmic carry-over left Kim reluctant to engage in intercourse for fear of replicating her brood mare status. She had to be made to realize that she and Bart had been given the opportunity to love again in much more enlightened times.

Even while Bob and Melody were conferring with us, they were playfully teasing one another. With their lively, competitive minds it was difficult to still them long enough to place them in trance.

While regressed, we learned that the man and wife in the present lifetime had been jealous brothers in old Spanish California. Although rivals for everything from horses to women, they had loved each other deeply and had died defending each other in a bloody vendetta. Our challenge was to help them realize that their love for each other in the present life experience must express itself in quite a different manner.

Julia and Mel were very frank with us. They had nothing good between them but sex. Their married life was an alternating series of depressions, boredom, and violent fights. And it seemed they were always broke and blaming the other for mismanagement of the budget. Nothing worked for them but the bedroom.

Through consultation and regression, we found them in New Orleans at the turn of the century. Julia was a prostitute; Mel was her brutal pimp. He had debauched her as a young girl and had made her his sexual slave. Although she despised him and had once even tried to kill him, she seemed to crave his style of lovemaking. It required a number of sessions to help this couple build their union on something more substantial than their bedsprings, but a realization of their own spiritual evolution helped them gain deeper value.

Louise was in a distraught condition when we first encountered her. A married woman, she had been involved with Steve (who was also married) for more than five years.

Through regression and consultation, Louise was enabled to see that although she and Steve had been happily married in a past life, they had fulfilled their karmic debts to each other and that in this lifetime they must work out previous situations with other partners. Painful as it may seem, in the present life experience, they must stay apart until they have worked out their growth potential with their new mates.

A tearful Katherine told us that she knew that she was ruining her son's life, but that she could not help herself. She had meddled in his relationships with women since he had been a teenager. She had been responsible for terminating two engagements and had been the direct cause of his divorce.

Through regression it was determined that Katherine and her son Philip had been man and wife in Paris in the 1890s. Theirs had been a pleasant marriage, complicated only by her jealousy of Philip, who had been a medical doctor with a great popularity among his female patients. Katherine had to be made to realize that jealousy could not be a part of their present relationship, which truly added a new dimension to their full experiencing of the circle of love.

Paula was in a state of distraction when she told us her story. Her husband Bill was driving her crazy with his total lack of trust. She was unable to go anywhere or to do anything without him. She had to provide him with a maddeningly detailed report of everything she did during the day when they were separated.

In consultation, we learned of their previous shared life experience of squalor and hard times in which Paula had had to support the crippled Bill by selling her sexual favors. Each night the tearful man would await her return in his wheelchair by the window and hear her agonized confessions. It was now Paula's challenge to assure Bill that she was a totally faithful wife in the present life experience. She at last persuaded Bill to attend a consultation with us, and he was able to see that his fears and his pain had been carried over from a previous lifetime. Their marriage has now truly begun to grow.

In comparing notes with other past life researchers, we have found an interesting kind of case study that we have all begun to confront. Leah and Eric are typical. In regression, we found that each of them claimed a first lifetime as a "being of light."

They saw themselves descending to Earth, then participating in a life experience as individuals engaged in social protest and spiritual preaching. In other lifetimes, they saw themselves working always for the betterment of humankind. Sometimes they were executed, burned at the stake for their efforts. Always, they were persecuted, but, undaunted, they continued to work with a devotion to good and spiritual evolution. In their present lifetimes as well, Leah and Eric have committed their life expressions to serving the highest spiritual and moral values.

EXPLORE YOUR OWN PAST LOVES

It has become tedious for me to argue whether past-life recall is pure fantasy or the actual memory of a prior existence. What is important is that, time and time again, I have witnessed men and women obtaining a definite and profound release from a present pain or phobia by reliving the origin of their problems in some real or alleged former existence.

Knowledge of previous existences is another form of awareness, and such an extended awareness can bring you much more than past-life memories—even more than the resolution of specific current problems. By exploring prior-life experiences, you may truly come to know yourself and to recall physical and mental skills that you may have mastered in other lifetimes. You may rediscover talents that can bring greater creativity to your present life. You may relearn how to become more efficient in the performance of daily tasks.

Interestingly, the extended awareness that you receive from past-life memories will serve to enhance all the pleasures that you derive through your senses in your present life. Your sight, your hearing, your touch, your smell, your taste will all become keener.

PAST-LIFE COMPANION EXERCISE

Lie or sit in a comfortable position and allow yourself to relax as completely as possible. Take a deep breath, hold it for the count of three, then slowly exhale. Repeat this procedure three times.

Visualize yourself sitting or reclining in your favorite place. Perhaps on a blanket on the beach. Perhaps on a rock beside a lovely mountain trail, on a park bench feeding the pigeons. On a comfortable couch in your own home. Wherever you choose to imagine yourself, next visualize that you have a companion with you.

Focus on this companion. Is the companion male or female? Study the color of hair, eyes, and complexion of your companion.

Watch your companion's facial expressions, posture, body movements. Are you relaxed with your companion? Is he or she relaxed with you?

If there is an instant rapport between you, take a few moments to learn why you feel so much at ease with one another.

If there is veiled hostility or distrust between you, take a few moments to contemplate the possible origin of those feelings.

Really focus now on your companion's face. Have you known this companion before in this present lifetime, or is this companion only a vaguely familiar stranger?

If you have visualized a person whom you know from your present-life experience, take a few moments to flow with your feelings. Who might this person represent?

It is quite likely that you have visualized your companion in contemporary clothing. If this is true, now that you are beginning to move into deeper thoughts about your companion, visualize him or her in clothing that you think most perfectly suits the individual. Permit this costuming to come from any period in history. Do not place any restraints on the flow that may now be coming to you.

Now visualize yourself with your companion in another time, another place. If your prior selection of beach, mountain trail, park bench, or home feels significant, however, stay with that environment. Imagine yourself taking your companion by the hand as you face a circle of friends and make an introduction along the following lines:

I would like you to meet my companion_____. We lived together in [country] in [year]. Our relationship was [marriage partners, lovers, siblings, friends, whatever].

Together, we faced [a situation of conflict] We shared bad times [reflect upon some] and good times [enjoy positive memories]. Our life together as companions ended when [remember the circumstances–death, separation, anger, whatever]. The most important lesson we learned together was [recall why you lived that past life together].

MEETING THE KARMIC COUNTERPART

When Frances and I were working one on one with consultees in daily regression sessions, we found it exceedingly effective to focus on the particular past life that we came to call the "Karmic Counterpart," that former existence that is directly responsible for the troublesome imbalance—the phobia, guilt, compulsion, illness, whatever—of the subject's present-life experience.

We are convinced that a resolution with the Karmic Counterpart is essential to proper balance in the present-life experience. We have always been distressed to encounter men and women who have been tormented by their maladjusted lives. Again and again in so many cases all we needed was one session with a subject in order to enable that person to see that he or she had been unknowingly permitting unconscious memories of a prior existence to ruin a fruitful relationship or a productive existence in the present-life experience. What was required was helping the consultee recognize the lessons that had left unlearned from that other time and assist him or her to begin at once to use the proper mental tools to make the present life truly workable.

Here is a technique to be used in meeting the Karmic Counterpart so that an effective dialogue may be established between the prior self and your present self.

Use *any* of the relaxation techniques that may have been successful for you in previous altered-states-of-consciousness exercises.

Once the body has been relaxed as deeply and completely as possible, permit the real you within the physical structure to become aware of a beautiful figure robed in violet standing near your sleeping body.

This beautiful figure is surrounded by an aura, a halo of golden light, and you know at once that you are beholding a guide who has come to take the *real you* out of your physical shell and to travel with you to a high dimension where you will be able to receive knowledge of a past life that you need to know about—a past life that has greatly influenced your present-life experience.

This will be a past life in which you will probably see a good many individuals who have come with you in your present life, to complete a task left unfinished, to learn a lesson left unaccomplished.

Whatever you see, it will be for your good and your gaining; and your guide will be ever near, allowing nothing to harm you. Your guide will be ever ready to protect you.

Permit your guide to take you by your hand and to lift the *real you* out of your body. Don't worry. You will always return to your body, but for now you are free to soar, totally liberated of time and space.

The swirling purple mist is moving all around you; hand in hand with your guide, you begin to move higher and higher.

You seem to be floating through space, moving gently through space, moving through all of time.

You know that you have the ability to move through time and to see a past life that you need to know about for your good and your gaining—a past life that will tell you very much about your present life.

This past life is primarily responsible for your present lot in life, for you are the counterbalance for your soul's previous expression.

Ahead of you, suspended in space, is a great golden door. And you know that when you step through that door you will be able to explore the past life or lives of your Karmic Counterpart.

You will be able to see the reasons why your soul chose the parents, the brothers or sisters, the friends, the mate, the nationality, the race, the sex, the talents, the occupation you have.

You will see the soul-chosen purpose for the agonies, troubles, pains, and griefs that have entered your life.

You will see what you presently need to accomplish to complete a work left unfinished, a lesson left unmastered.

Now your guide is ushering you to the great golden door. The door is opening, and you step inside.

You see yourself as you were when you were a child in that life.

If it is for your good and your gaining, you are able to know what country you are living in—as you would understand it today—and what period of time you are living in—as you would understand it today.

You see the color of your eyes, your hair, your skin. You see clearly what sex you are.

Now see your body clothed. See yourself in characteristic clothing for that time. See clearly what is on your feet.

A man and a woman are now approaching you. Look at their eyes. It is the man and woman who were your father and mother in *that* life.

Understand what kind of relationship you had with them. Did they love you? Understand you? Reject you?

If they did love and understand you, did you always wish that they might have loved and understood you more?

And now, for your good and your gaining look at their eyes and see if either of them came with you in your present-life experience—to complete work left unfinished, to master a lesson left unlearned.

Someone else is approaching you, and you see that it is a brother or a sister with whom you were very close. Look at this person's eyes.

This is a brother or sister who *loved* you and *supported* you.

And now, looking into their eyes, see if that beloved brother or sister came with you in your present life—to complete work left undone, to finish a lesson left unlearned.

In that same lifetime you are growing older, moving into young adulthood, and you see yourself performing some favorite activity: a game, a sport, a hobby that became so much a part of your life *then* that it has, on one level of consciousness, affected your life today.

You see yourself performing that activity, and you understand how it has been impressed on the life pattern you exercise today.

You are now beginning to see clearly and to understand what *work* you did in that life—how you survived, how you provided for yourself or for others, how you spent your days.

As you move away from your work situation, you are beginning to feel the *vibrations of love* moving all around you. You are aware of someone standing there, to your left, in the shadows.

You are feeling love—warm, peaceful sensations of love—moving all around you, as you realize that standing there in the shadows is the person whom you loved most in that lifetime.

Look at the eyes. Feel the love flowing toward you from those beautiful eyes of your beloved.

Look at the smile of recognition on those lips as the beloved one sees you and begins to move toward you.

This is the one with whom you shared your most intimate moments—your hopes, your dreams, your moments of deepest love. And yes, your sorrows, your hurts, your moments of deepest pain.

This is the one who always cared, who always loved and supported you.

Go to those arms again. Feel those beloved arms around you. Feel those lips on yours again.

Now, for your good and your gaining look at the eyes. See if this beloved one came with you in your present-life experience.

See if your love, like a golden cord, has stretched across time, space, generations, years, to entwine you again in the same beautiful love vibrations.

See if you have come together again to work out a task left incomplete, a lesson left unlearned.

You are growing older in that life. See now the one whom you *married* in that life. Was it the one you loved most? Or was that beloved one taken from you by death or by circumstances?

If the one you see before you now was not the one you loved most, then looking at the eyes, see for your good and your gaining the person you *did* marry. And see for your good and your gaining if that person came with you in your present life to complete work left undone, a lesson left unlearned.

If you had *children* in that life, see them now. See their eyes looking up at you. Feel their little hands on your fingers. Feel the love flowing from them.

Did they grow older with you? Or were they taken from you by death or by circumstances?

Look at their eyes, and for your good and your gaining see if any of those children came with you in your present-life experience to complete a lesson left unlearned, to be with you again in your love vibration.

Now see scenes from that life that you need to remember for your proper soul evolution.

See scenes that will trigger memories that will help you in your present-life experience.

See scenes that will show you clearly how certain patterns were formed and then have intruded, both positively and negatively, into your present-life experience.

These are scenes you need to remember, but you will see them in a detached manner. You will feel neither guilt nor shame. You will feel neither pride nor ego pleasure.

You will understand them—*why* they happened. You will understand these acts so that your soul may grow and gain.

And now, for your good and your gaining, witness the moment of your *death* in *that* life.

Perhaps you weren't ready for death, perhaps you fought against it, cursed it. But understand *why* your soul withdrew its energy at that time.

See who was with you at that last moment. Was the one you loved most there? Your family? Your children? Or were you all alone? Did you face that last moment all alone?

See your spirit rising from its physical shell. See yourself being met by your very own angel guide, the same guide who is with you from lifetime to lifetime.

With a flash of insight your angel guide is showing you *why* you lived that life and why you lived it with those with whom you did.

You see clearly *why* you had to come again to put on the fleshly clothes of Earth.

You see *why* you had to come in your present life as the person you are now.

You see *why* certain people from that life have come with you again to complete work left undone, to master a lesson left unlearned.

You are beginning to awaken, feeling very, very good and very, very positive.

You are filled with a beautiful, glowing sense of love.

You are filled with the positive knowledge that you will be able to accomplish so much more good and gaining toward your true mission now that you are filled with awareness of your Karmic Counterpart.

Now you understand how that lifetime has been affecting your present life.

Now you understand so very much more of the great pattern of your lifetimes.

Now you understand so very much more of the great pattern of how you have interacted with the Love Force.

And you know that your guide will aid you, will assist you in completing your mission, in accomplishing what you truly came here to do.

Awaken filled with positive feelings of love, wisdom, and knowledge. Awaken feeling very, very good in the body, mind, and spirit. Awaken feeling better than you have felt in weeks, in months, in years. Awaken filled with love.

12

STRENGTHEN YOUR OWN LOVE FORCE

The Love Force has a sound. I have heard it internally for many years. My wife Frances has heard it since childhood—and so have thousands of men and women who have written to tell us that they, too, have experienced this internal manifestation of the love energy. Perhaps you have also heard this high-pitched hum or whistle within your own being.

The compelling sound of the Love Force actually externalized for us in the King's Chamber of the Great Pyramid on November 2, 1982.

The Great Pyramid of Giza—the stuff of which legends, dreams, fables, and alternate realities are fashioned—stood there before us like an archetype from the unconscious that had suddenly been made manifest in the ancient desert sands of Egypt. Half-remembered lines from inspired poetry, the tributes of emperors and kings, the awe-struck journals of early explorers, and the cinematic cameras of a dozen epics have all paid tribute to this most magnificent of structures.

Amazingly, we had awakened in our Holiday Inn (a seeming

anachronism that prevented us from entering total culture shock in Egypt), looked outside, and beheld the Great Pyramid and its two smaller siblings. Somehow it was as if we were gazing into a time tunnel: automobiles and modern enterprise on one side of the tunnel, camels and genius from a mysterious antiquity on the other.

Frances' guide had told us that we must be in the King's Chamber of the Great Pyramid on November 2, 1982. Why, he did not say. But since this was the entity who has provided us with telephone numbers, street addresses, and any number of important items of business with an eerie accuracy, I did not ask.

I could never have guessed what was to transpire on that morning. I would never have been so presumptuous as to have requested the kind of demonstration we received.

Joy Burton, our tour director, had arranged for us to enter the pyramid at 8:00 A.M., one hour before the other tourists would be permitted to enter.

I felt at one with a thousand vibrations of those who had entered these stone portals before me. My God! I was actually going inside the Great Pyramid! I was really doing it myself and not vicariously letting Charlton Heston, Harrison Ford, or Cecil B. DeMille do it for me.

One does not simply *walk* into the King's Chambers. You climb—*crawl*—on a steep incline through a very small tunnel for what seems to be at least a hundred yards. You then emerge into a larger chamber in which, you are relieved to note, you can again stand upright. You do, however, have even steeper steps to climb until you at last enter the King's Chamber.

If you expect a movie-set tomb when you enter the chamber, you will be disappointed. All the glorious golden artifacts were removed a long time ago. All that remains is this bare room with an open sarcophagus at one end.

I must emphasize that simply *being there* was enough for me.

But since we were standing in what is probably the single most mystical pilgrimage point for metaphysicians on this entire planet, I felt compelled to lead a very brief creative visualization of a possible past life that our souls might have led in ancient Egypt.

Fran requested a silent meditation.

It was when I turned to touch Frances' right forefinger with my own that it happened.

As I held my forefinger against hers, *the* sound filled the chamber: the sound that we have termed the "Star People" signal.*

Let me explain briefly. In *The Star People* we mention that the Star People "experience a buzzing or a clicking sound or a high-pitched mechanical whine in the ears prior to, or during, some psychic event or warning of danger." Frances and I, and a good many of those gathered in the King's Chamber that morning, have heard that signal all of our lives.

Now, at the touch of my right forefinger on Frances' right forefinger, the sound of that same high-pitched mechanical whine filled the room.

At first I thought that only I was aware of the sound, since I know that when I hear it in traffic, the supermarket checkout line, or walking on a street, I am the only one who hears it. Later, a number of others laughingly confessed that they, too, believed themselves to be the only ones experiencing the familiar signal.

But the sound was definitely externalized. All around me I noticed members of our Star People gathering uncomfortably turning their heads and scrunching their shoulders toward their ears.

How would I describe the sound? Did you see *2001: A Space Odyssey?* Do you remember the piercing sound when the monolith was uncovered on the moon and beamed its signal toward Jupiter?

You may have heard the sound in *E.T., The Extraterrestrial*, when E.T. touches his right forefinger to Elliot's right forefinger.

But on November 2, 1982, the sound that we had previously experienced only internally had now externalized in the King's Chamber. I cannot think of a more convincing sign of confirmation than each of us hearing loudly and externally the same sound at the same exact pitch as the mechanical whining sound that we so often hear internally when we are receiving psychic messages.

Always the researcher as well as the participant, I methodically checked each of the half-dozen tape recorders in the chamber. I put

---

* In the Steigers' book *The Star People*, Frances Steiger defines a Star Person as one who has the ability to attain the perspective of one who views the planet from a universal standpoint, understanding that all life is one upon its surface, interrelated and symbiotically dependent, existing with a purpose, a most beautiful and Harmonious Plan. Being a Star Person is being a transcended Humane Being and showing humaneness in all that you do when related to others.

my ear to the dim electrical bulb. None of the camera batteries or recorders were emitting anything other than their normal clicks and buzzes. The sound was not coming from anywhere in particular. *It was coming from all around us.*

Each of the operative tape recorders impressed the sound into their own mechanism. We have a full audio record of the signal as it rose and fell for the entire forty-five minutes in which we occupied the King's Chamber.

I must say that the experience caused me to rededicate my life to that which Fran has termed "Star Consciousness." Such consciousness requires that one develop an awareness of his or her potential abilities as a sovereign identity and yet retain the perspective of one who views the planet from the stars and understands that *all* life is One upon its surface.

Frances has always said that this is the sound on which "they"—the multidimensional beings of Love and Light—enter our sphere of reality. This is the sound to which one might attune himself or herself in order to establish a greater contact with higher intelligences and with the very essence of the Love Force that emanates from the Source of All-That-Is.

I truly hope that each reader of this book shall one day have the exhilarating experience of hearing the sound of the Love Force, either internally or externally; but I surely do not wish anyone to put off the strengthening of his or her own love energy until such a manifestation might occur. In the nineteenth-century, English novelist Maria Jane Jewsbury wrote:

> *Love is the purification of the heart from self. It strengthens and ennobles the character, gives higher motive and nobler aim to every action of life, and makes both man and woman strong, noble, and courageous. The power of love truly and devotedly is the noblest gift with which a human being can be endowed; but it is a sacred fire that must not be burned to idols.*

I offer the exercises in this concluding chapter with my earnest desire for your success in fashioning a Love Force that will be self-nurturing, yet unselfish; self-protective, yet giving; self-fulfilling, yet generous.

DEVELOPING A GREATER HARMONY WITH THE ENERGIES OF NATURE

... If we wish to make a religion of love ... we must take universal good, not universal powers, for the object of our religion. ... There would not be a universe worshipped, but a universe praying; and the flame of the whole fire, the whole seminal and generative movement of nature, would be the love of God ... it would be really love and not something wingless called by that name.

George Santayana, *Obiter Scripta*

Take a comfortably deep breath, hold it for the count of three, then release it. Repeat this three times.

Begin to look toward the north. Let your eyes go to the far, far horizon of the north. Begin to feel yourself *growing* as you look toward the north.

Visualize yourself stretching upward, as if you are, perhaps, a tall redwood tree. Stretch your arms out in front of you as if they are limbs stretching forth.

Imagine that you can touch the far horizon of the north. Then turning slowly, imagine that your arms stretch out and touch the horizon, the great pole of the horizon, as if you can brush the very farthest reaches of the horizon with your fingertips, as you move slowly around. Perhaps you are touching a forest, or a cloud, or the ocean. Perhaps you are touching the waters of a lake. Perhaps you are touching grasses on a rolling plane.

Wherever you are, as you move slowly with your great arms stretching from horizon to horizon, let the Earth Mother know that you are aware of her. Bless her and all that you touch. Feel the energy moving out from you, blessing all that you touch. Feel the blessing returning to you.

Keep your eyes open as you move counter-clockwise. Moving counter-clockwise, feel your fingertips brush the farthest reaches that you can see with your eyes. As far as you can see with your eyes, *touch* with your fingertips.

Now close your eyes. Close your eyes and know that you are a focal point. There is the great Earth Mother all around you; there is the great Sky Father above you. All around you are energies seen and unseen, felt and only guessed at.

You, through your mind, constitute the focal point that touches the universe, that caresses the Earth Mother. Open all of your senses to receive the blessing that the Earth Mother sends back to you. Feel and know yourself to be at the center of a great benevolent energy, which is consecrated by all that surrounds you.

DEVELOPING A GREATER HARMONY WITH COSMIC INTELLIGENCE AND PROJECTING LOVE TO ANOTHER

We are shaped and fashioned by what we love–Goethe

How can you become more conscious of your identification with the intelligence that fills space?

When you sit in quiet meditation, you are, in fact, attuning yourself to this cosmic intelligence. Every time you spend a few minutes in quiet attunement with the Cosmos, you are helping to undo the restricting attitude of separateness, and you are permitting love to flow more easily through you.

A good exercise to repeat on a daily basis to demonstrate repeatedly your ability to join the seen and the unseen is to stand with your arms stretched forward, your palms down, then intone the universal sound "OM" in a long, drawn-out chant. O-O-O-O-M-M-M.

Repeat this until you can actually feel tingling in the palms of your hands. Until the skin actually picks up auditory vibrations.

Then begin to project another type of energy toward your palms. Try to project a life force to your palms. Visualize the life force passing through your fingers, moving out to the palms of your hands. Focus on this until you begin to feel a tingling sensation—almost as if electrical vibrations are moving through you.

Next, begin to feel an actual palpable force moving out of your palms. Visualize a violet ball of energy, hovering just beyond the palms of your hands. Visualize this as a great energy of love.

Begin to project this Love Force to others.

Visualize the violet sphere moving through the walls, through the ceiling, through space, and see it enveloping someone whom you are visualizing in your mind. Visualize that violet globe of light surrounding that individual with love.

This is a way to establish a telepathic connection. This is a way to cause someone to begin to think favorably about you. This is a good way of causing someone in whom you may have a romantic interest to feel your love.

FILLING YOURSELF WITH ANGELIC LOVE

Love is an image of God, and not a lifeless image, but the living essence of the divine nature, which beams full of all goodness–Martin Luther.

Frances has developed a beautiful technique to manifest the blending of mortal spirit with that of unconditional, angelic love. This exercise produces excellent results in elevating your Love Force to its highest levels.

[The following induction may be used to help intensify this creative visualization. As previously suggested in this book, you may engage the assistance of a trusted individual to read the induction and the experience to you, or you may previously record the instructions in your own voice.]

Imagine that you are walking down a peaceful country lane toward a soft, green area of countryside. You know that this is a beautiful, tranquil place. You know that you will be safe and protected here. You know that this is a holy place, surrounded by the golden energy of unconditional love.

You find a lush, grassy area—a place that feels special and right to you—and you lie down. The grass is like a soft, fluffy blanket beneath you, and you nestle comfortably down into it. You know that this is a perfect place to rest, to find peace, to enjoy nature. It is, so lovely, so peaceful.

Stretch out and begin to take nice, long, deep breaths . . . nice, slow, deep breaths. Relax here in your grassy, soft bed. The sound of a nearby bubbling brook adds to the beauty of this place, this holy place. The trickling water lapping over the rocks will help to lull you to sleep.

As you lie on your back gazing upward, you notice that the sky is the clearest blue . . . with fluffy, white clouds spotting it now and then. It is, so peaceful, so wonderful. Relax. Your body is falling asleep. You are becoming more and more relaxed, and you find yourself breathing deeper and deeper, slower and slower.

Your taut muscles expand, then gently relax. It is, so peaceful, so wonderful, so soothing lying here resting and watching the clouds.

Your body is falling asleep, but your mind will remain aware. The soothing, gentle warmth of an afternoon sun feels like loving, warm fingers soothingly massaging the muscles of your body and helping you to fall asleep.

You can feel the soft, warm sun caressing, soothing, the muscles in your feet, your toes, your heels.

The warm fingers are moving, massaging the muscles in your ankles, your calves, warming, soothing . . . relaxing all the muscles of your legs. Healing, soothing warmth moves deep into your knees, your thighs, your hips . . . moving deep into the joints . . . healing, warming, releasing all tensions.

You are so relaxed, so peaceful, as the gentle, soothing warmth moves into your abdomen, deep into the lowest part of your back, into your chest, your shoulders . . . permitting all of your muscles to relax, all of your body to fall into a deep, deep sleep.

Nothing you hear will disturb you. Any sound that you might hear—a cough, a sniffle, a closing door, someone's voice—will only help you to drift deeper asleep.

Now the soothing, gentle, warm fingers of the Sun slide up your spine and relax every muscle of your neck, your scalp. All tensions in your neck and scalp are relaxed. Your body sleeps . . . your body sleeps. Nothing can disturb you. Nothing can distress you. You are at peace. You are at one with yourself.

Even now, as you lie here in peace and tranquility, you are feeling the three highest vibrations of this plane of existence begin to enter your body. Feel now the beautiful vibration of *love* move warmly through your body. Feel the gentle vibration of *wisdom* move through your very essence. Feel the pulsating vibration of *knowledge* move through your central self. Feel your entire being vibrate with Love, Wisdom, and Knowledge.

See yourself now clothed in a beautiful violet robe. You are standing before the pulsating Ocean of Life. Now reach into your robe, just over your heart, and remove a drinking cup. Hold it heavenward and mentally shout up the words: "Love! Love! Love!"

As you watch the sky above you, you see a beautiful love vibration gathering in each of the four corners of the heavens. One golden ray comes from the north, another from the south, another from the east, and another from the west.

They meet, merge, and form one almost blinding ray of golden light.

This ray is filled with heavenly love, angelic love, and it is beaming down to you.

It is splashing into your cup, filling it up as it transforms itself from light energy to silvery nectar.

It flows into your cup until it runs over the brim and anoints you.

Now lower the cup to your lips and drink the Golden nectar. Drink it all. Drink down this heavenly love. Feel how it glows and warms every part of your body.

Put your cup back inside your robe and enjoy the warmth.

Next, feel yourself begin to float. You are rising higher and higher.

As you look up, you see a huge, glowing cloud descending to meet you. It is white, tinged with gold.

It comes nearer. When you reach it, you climb aboard and rise even higher.

You are rising above Earth. You are rising above the clouds. You are rising higher and higher.

You move beyond the Earth, beyond the stars, beyond this dimension. You rise above nine levels to reach the beautiful crystal city in the sky.

Step off the cloud and see before you a crystal river of cleansing, sacred, holy water.

This holy, healing water cleanses within as well as without. It removes all scars, hurts, pains, regrets, and burdens, and it leaves you clean.

Wash yourself. Dip your whole body into the water. It is the perfect temperature, and it rises only as high as your heart.

If you have any troublesome or annoying habits or addictions, wash them away, too; and watch them float away down stream.

Then, clean and pure as a newborn baby, get out of the holy, healing water, the inner baptism, and walk to the opposite shore.

It is at this time that you can make decisions without regret. If you have any problem you wish to solve, a decision you need to make, leave it floating on the water.

As you stand on the opposite shore, see it bobbing on the holy water, awaiting your decision.

You are now facing the problem, but you are detached, separate from it. You have severed its emotional attachment to you.

Know that God is goodness!

Face the problem floating on the water and say this: "In the name of God, if it is for my good and my gaining, rise!

"In the name of God, if it is *not* for my good and my gaining, sink and be gone from me!"

If the problem rises, return to the water, snatch it from the air, and clutch it to your bosom. It is for your good and your gaining.

You may test the problem again in the same manner whenever you wonder whether or not you should continue to carry the problem with you.

If the problem sinks and is gone from you, let it go. Do not return to the water. The problem may be for another to bear, but it is not for you.

Once you have made your decision—or if there is no problem to test—turn away from the holy, healing water and climb the opposite bank. Walk up a grassy knoll.

As you climb toward its top, program yourself positively. Be truly proud of your efforts toward self-improvement. Vow to move away from any negative, unwanted habits.

Now, at the top of the hill, you see a beautiful, golden chalice, bedecked with jewels. The huge chalice is filled to the top with a milky, pink substance. It is a distillation of the highest love available—God's love!

You have been filled with angelic love.

You have cleansed yourself in the crystal river, washing yourself within as well as without. You have made any necessary decisions without regret with divine help.

Now drink from the golden chalice of God's love. Drink every drop of it.

Vow from this moment on to be as a kettle or teapot of unconditional love.

Whenever you interact with any living thing, picture yourself as a tea kettle of love, complete with a spout. Periodically imagine yourself pouring out unconditional love on a person, animal, or plant.

Unconditional heavenly love flows in through the top of your head, filling you totally, to the very brim. You pour out love to all of life through the spout, where your heart is.

Every drop that is given from the spout is immediately replenished through the top.

Remember that just as it is extremely difficult to fill a teapot to its brim by pouring in the spout, so it is nearly impossible to be filled with earthly love through the heart. The deep, inner hunger can be filled only by God's love, which comes in through the top.

Become an instrument of God's perfect love. If someone rejects your love, your sharing, do not feel hurt or rejected. You will be instantly filled through the top with God's love.

Never give love expecting a return from earthly love. The love of a mate, a child, a parent, or a friend is a bonus while on the Earth plane. But that deep longing can be satisfied only by God's love. One should never expect to fill his kettle from the spout.

When you reach a greater understanding, you will be able to image your "spiritual tea kettle" on even inanimate things. All will be in balance, for you will be vibrating with the highest attunement in the universe—love!

Now, set the chalice down and once again reach inside your robe. Remove a key from its resting place near your heart.

Look toward the horizon. See looming up from the midst of the crystal city the great spires of the magnificent golden temple. Rush to the temple. You are now prepared to enter into its vibration.

See before you a gigantic golden door, nine feet high, three feet wide.

Your key fits its lock. Open the door.

Enter and discover the three highest vibrations—love, wisdom, knowledge.

Awaiting you within are the angels and the soul-essences of holy men and women from all times and cultures.

CHANNELING THE LOVE FORCE
FOR TRUE SEXUAL SATISFACTION

To love one who loves you, to admire one who admires you . . . is exceeding the limit of human joy; it is stealing fire from heaven—Madame de Giradin

Frances has channeled a simple mental exercise through which you can master control of the universal energy and focus it through your own personal energy system. You have the ability to open, to magnify, and to energize your seven chakras, thereby balancing your universe—your temple within—mentally, physically, and spiritually.

On the physical plane you can easily feel the immediate effect of the universal energy when it is being directed into your own first energy system, your sexual chakra.

Close your eyes and quiet your entire body for one or two minutes. Mentally imagine the gathering of the energy that exists in all of matter. See it moving toward your crown chakra. Imagine it coming to you and entering your head. Feel it traveling down your spine and bursting into your first chakra, your sexual region.

Again, *imagine* it, *gather* it, *channel* it down your spine. Feel it burst into your sexual chakra.

Again, *imagine, channel, feel,* and *let it burst* into your first chakra.

Do this over and over, permitting waves of energy to enter you, to flow down you and through you and burst into your first chakra. This will produce pleasurable feelings.

This is the easiest area in which to feel the immediate effect of energy, for it is a most sensitive zone. It is an energy center that demands, even commands, our attention throughout our lives, for it is a very important area for the existence of animal life on our planet. It controls the male and female reproductive system so that we replicate ourselves. By channeling the energy into your first chakra, your sexual zone, you will learn how to master the channeling of energy into and through your remaining chakras, thereby raising them into finer attunement.

In this, the world of polarities where energy manifests positively or negatively due to our own direction, the first chakra is the easiest of the seven chakras to energize. The need for new life favors this energy, but since it is the easiest to energize, it is the hardest to control. But control it you must; the energy that can be created by this center, if channeled negatively, can result in great destruction, sexual perversion, frustrating lust, and greed, with ensuing anger and chaos.

The heart chakra is an energy system that, when mastered with love, will permit you positive control over your sexual chakra, for it aids all chakras. Using the heart chakra and the sexual chakra together causes the energy to be governed positively, magnifying it to its fullest capacity, intensifying it to its greatest height.

This is why we enjoy sex far more with someone we *love*, why it is more beautiful and complete. And that is also why sex becomes mechanical with those we do not love, for the act then becomes only a form of masturbation to release the existing energy in this center through robotlike manipulation.

Experiencing the unconditional love energy in the heart chakra is a beautiful feeling in itself. Blending it with the sexual energy magnifies your sexual enjoyment. With continued practice the ultimate pleasure will result, for it becomes more perfected, more controlled.

Close your eyes, quiet your entire body, relaxing it from head to toe for a few minutes.

Now imagine above you the love energy within all that exists. See it gathering from the north, coming to the center of the heavens directly above you. (Imagining the energy aids in your tapping it, using it, and eventually controlling it.) Now imagine it coming from the south, from the east, and from the west, gathering together, blending into one glowing ball of bright, golden energy.

Imagine this energy coming down toward you, coming down and pouring into your head, entering your crown chakra.

Think positively; think of the most positive of all things, the highest thought available to you. Think of unconditional love for all living things, nonjudgmental love, and feel this energy travel down your spine positively, like a thick, warming, glowing, tingling energy—filling you, making you feel complete, whole.

Imagine it filling your heart completely.

Imagine before you the one you love. Now permit the energy to continue to travel down your spine and enter into your sexual region, your first chakra. Permit it to fill this region.

Feel it glow. Permit the two energy systems to vibrate together—your heart chakra imagining your loved one before you, and your sexual chakra. Feel it harmonize, blend, and glow as one.

Again gather the energy, and notice how it continues to collect and to pour in waves into your crown chakra. See and feel the waves of energy enter you. Think of unconditional love for all living things. Feel it fill your heart. Think of your love. Feel it enter your sexual region.

Continue this process over and over. Feel how your sexual energy has been modified, magnified, glorified.

Throughout the day and into the early evening hours—or whenever you wish to prepare for sexual enjoyment—perform this mental exercise of blending the heart chakra with the sexual chakra while imagining your mate before you. This should be repeated five or six times at least. You will notice how it takes less time for you to imagine, manifest, and feel the energy travel through your body. You will also notice how it takes less time to perform the entire exercise and how you are becoming more proficient at it.

Moments before sexual intercourse, perform this mental exercise to the fullest strength, permitting it to glow full within you, vibrating your heart and sexual areas to their strongest, most complete capacity. Continue the process throughout the entire sexual act. Feel the waves of energy entering your heart and your sexual areas, while expressing unconditional, all-encompassing love for your mate. Feel the waves of energy gathering and welling up in your heart and your sexual areas and becoming one mighty force. Continue this process until you desire to release all of the energy collected within you. Then do so with love.

Obviously, if both partners practice this imagery together, the energy they both generate and exchange with each other becomes so intense that the most beautiful of all sexual feelings will manifest themselves—love and sexuality, the blending of the divine with the material. When the two are balanced, total, positive, complete, and harmonious, they are wondrous to behold.

TRANSMITTING THE LOVE FORCE AROUND THE WORLD

The greatest happiness of life is the conviction that we are loved, loved for ourselves, or rather loved in spite of ourselves.
Victor Hugo

I hope that you have already noticed that when you give unconditional love its energy can never be depleted, for you receive it anew from above. You can never receive imbalance, hatred, envy, or jealousy when you are filled with love. You can never be touched by negative vibrations when you are filled with the Love Force.

Neither can you fill yourself with love and hold it within your being. You must pour it forth upon the world or it will stagnate.

If you bottle up love within you, you will find that it simply cannot keep. It will soon sour. Love must be given so that you may receive it afresh.

Even now as you read these words, feel unconditional love, nonjudgmental love, pouring into your body.

Feel it entering your crown chakra and filling up your entire physical vessel. Be aware of it filling your feet, your ankles, your legs, your hips, your stomach, chest, and back. Feel it entering your arms. Sense it moving up your spine. Know that it has entered your neck, your shoulders, your head. Understand that you are now filled to the crown of your head. Be aware that you are vibrating, glowing with unconditional love.

Now imagine that there is a golden pyramid above your head, directly over your crown chakra. Understand that this pyramid collects vibrations of love from the Source, then channels them directly into your crown chakra. Realize with all your essence that you have now banished all negativity and that your psyche and your physical body are now balanced.

Image someone whom you love. Visualize a golden beam of light from your heart chakra streaking across space and touching that loved one at the heart chakra area. Feel strongly the link-up.

Now imagine that you are sending love around the Earth. Visualize that you will touch all those men and women who are depressed, who are feeling unloved, who are feeling imbalanced. All those who are imprisoned by negativity may reach out and make contact with the beautiful energy of unconditional love that you are sending around the planet.

Feel yourself pouring out unconditional love from your heart chakra. See it streaming all over the Earth. Know that it is touching the lonely, the despondent, the bitter, the negative. Know that it is uplifting their spirits. Know that it is helping raise their consciousness. Know that it is balancing their energies.

Be aware that you are giving and receiving anew the unconditional love vibration. Feel the energy, the strength, the God-vibration within the love frequency. Know that the more love you pour forth from your heart chakra, the more love from the Source you will receive through your crown chakra. The more you transmit, the more you will be energized.

Practice this broadcasting of the love vibration on a regular basis, and no negativity can ever pervade you, can ever harm you, can ever hurt you. If you truly fill yourself with unconditional love from the Source of All-That-Is, negativity will never again be able even to touch your life.

Give and receive love, and you will immediately become a positive conductor for the Love Force itself, sharing in all its unparalleled glory and awesome power.

INDEX

Altered state technique for contact with other side, 110–13
Ancient Leaves, 58
Angelic love, filling self with, 196–200
Angels, supposed visits from, 160–65
  on farm, 160–62
  soldier in desert, 164–65
Apollo 14, 70
Apparition of ghosts, cases, 4–6, 98–100
Apparitions at moment of death, 89–95
  features of, 92
  vs. ghost, 92
  as image implant, 95
  nature of, questions about, 91
  verification, 91, 92
Apportation case, 140–42
Association for the Psychophysiological Study of Sleep, 43
  Astral projection, 1–3, 73–87
  color meditation for:
    blue, 85
    gold, 84
    green, 84
    imagined demonstration, 86–87
    impurities, 85
    and Love Force, 84
    lungs, 84
    oxygen, 84–85
    red–orange, 84–85
    rose, 83–84
    temples, priests, and so forth, 86
    violet, 85–86
    yellow–orange, 85
  in danger, 74
  Egypt, 74
  and hypnagogic state, 80–82
    doubles, case, 80–82
  in mystic religions, 74
  near-death experience, 82
  orgasms, 79–80
  rate of, 73
  and sex, 74–78
  in West, 74

Barker, Lois, 96
Bernard, Eugene E., 73
Between Two Worlds, 151
Black bird of happiness, case, 22–23
Blanchard, Jerry, 4–6

Blanchard, Opal, 4–6
Blanton, Smiley, 18
Brant, Carlyle, 1–3
Brant, Mina, 1–3
Burton, Joy, 191

Cefalu, Joseph Friend, 63
Center of the Cyclone, The, 166
Christianson, Claudia, 46
Christianson, Gerald, 47
Cocreating with light beings, 172
Contact with spirits, dealing with:
  medium, establishing identity by, 107
  messages for, 107
  questions, 107
  welcomes, 106
Cosmic intelligence, harmony with, 195–96
Couples, telepathic bond in, 65–67
  cry for help, 66–67
Creator, expansion of, 133

"Daemonic, The: Love and Death," 15–16
"Daemonic," nature of, 15–16
Death, apparition cases, 4–8
Deceased spouses, return of, 144–47
De Giradin, Mme., 200
De La Rivera, Anna, 149–50
Demon lovers, examples, 16–18
Direct-voice sittings, 108–09
  identification of spirits, 109
  light, 109
  questions for spirits, 109
  trance, 109
  whispers, 109
Disturbing dreams, dissipation of, 58
  gold, 58
  head, 58
  heart, 58
  violet light, 58
Divine beings, union with, 165–70
  contact ritual, 168–70
  environment for, 169–70
  Frances Steiger, angel to, 166
  PSE evaluation of statements, 167
  thought control, 170
Dream Lab, Maimonides Medical Center, 42–43, 46–47
Dream, recall of, 57
Dream telepathy, emotional ties of, 43–44
  alarm case, 44–45
  shared dreams, 45–47
  studies about, 43–44
Dudevant, Mme., 20

Energies, 133–36
  chaotic, 133–34
  contact, hazards of, 135
  harmonious, 133–34
  and heaven, 134
  and hell, 134
  high-level being, contacts with, 136
  and limbo, 134–36
    contact with, 136
  low-level contacts:
    block to, 136
    signs of, 136–37
  and physical death, 134
  Scriptures on, 136
  unconditional love, 135
Erickson, Forrest L., 167
Eros, frustration of, 16
Essenes, 177
ESP:
  early development of, 36
  and sex drive, 10
ET The Extraterrestrial, 192
Eternal Flame of Isis, 35–36
  burning of paper, 36
  prayer for, 36

Females as receivers, 10
Firkins, Oscar W., 3
Flandre, Charles, 92–93
Flandre, Laura, 92–93
Foder, Nandor, 130, 151
Footfalls on the Boundary of Another World, 97
Fox, Oliver, 75, 77

Gays as seers, 25–26
Gilroy, William H., 63
Glass of water exercise, 71–72
Gnostic Gospels, 177
Goethe, 195
Great Pyramid at Giza:
  and higher beings, 193
  King's Chamber, 191
  and love, 193
  and Love Force sound, 190–93
  supposed observation of, 192–93
Great Silence, 55

Halpern, Steven, 58
Harbot, Esther, 93–95
Harbot, William, 93–95

Haunted house in Lincoln, Nebraska:
  apparition, 128–29
  manifestations, 126, 127
  murder scene, 126–130
  psychokinesis on door, 126–27
Haunting by dead wife, case, 10–13
  communications from, 13
Honorton, Charles, 43
Hugo, Victor, 203
Humility, importance of, 172
Hunter, apparition of wife of to save life, case, 13–15
Hurt:
  student, case, 64–65
  telepathic projection of, 64–65
Hypnagogic state, 8

Immortality: The Scientific Evidence, 95
Invisible strangler, case, 131–32

Jealous spirits, 138ff.
Jewsbury, Maria Jane, 193
Jonsson, Olof, 70–72

Kelley, Georgia, 86
Krippner, Stanley, 43, 47, 67
Kübler-Ross, Elisabeth, 165

Lang, Andrew, 91
Lauer, Dorothy Spence, 38
Laverty, Owen, 9–10
Lilly, John, 166
Love, dream vision seeking:
  crown chakra, 55–57
  effects, 56–57
  heart chakra, 57
  images, 56–57
  prayer, 56
  ritual, 54–56
  source, 56
Love, effects, 18–19
Love Force:
  broadcast, 203–05
  nature, 3–4
Love or Perish, 18
Love projection, 195–96
  and OM, 195
Love vision, attaining, 58–61
  crystal, 60
  guide, 59
  locations, 59–60
  and Love Force, 59
  recollection, 61

  violet light, 59
Lover, true feelings of, reception, 69
Lovers, dreamed/precognitized, 50–55
Lovers, reincarnated, 177–89
  emotional release, 178
  exploration, 182–83
  karmic counterpart, meeting of, 184–89
  karmic debts, 177–78
  previous companion visualization, 183–84
  sense enhancement, 183
Luther, Martin, 196

Males as senders, 10
Mandel, William, 8–10
May, Rollo, 15
Mayer, Victor, 6–8
Mediumship:
  automatic writing, 102–03
  expectancy method, 101–02
  and Frances Steiger, 100
  group, expansion of, 103
  practice, 100–01
  receivers, 103–04
  seance room, 101
  senders, 103–04
  telepathy exercise, 104
Meyers, W. H., 73
Mind Travelers, The, 79
Misguided marriage, paranormal case, 9–10
Mitchell, Edgar, 70
Morning prayer, 172
Muldoon, Sylvan, 75
Mystery schools, Egyptian, 177

Natural harmony, ritual:
  Earth Mother, 194–95
  Sky Father, 194
Negative entities, prayer against, 170
Negativity, transforming, 157–59
  assertions, 158
  circle building, 158–59
  and Love Force, 157–59
  loved persons, 158
  OM, 157
  sparks, 157
  visions, 157

Oberlin, John Frederick, 97–98
  visits to by dead wife, 97, 98
Obiter Scripta, 194
O'Donnell, Brian, 10

Oltersdorf, Gina, 160
Oltersdorf, Julie, 160
OM, 157, 195
Ouija boards, 143–44
Out-of-body experiences. *See* Astral projections
Owen, Robert Dale, 97

Pendragon, John, 23–24
Petrarch, 19
Physical phenomena:
  apports, 110
  conditions for, 110
  objects, 110
  ouija boards, 109
  planchettes, 109
  rules, 109
  table tilting, 109
Pilgrim, Martha, 13
Poltergeists:
  attacks on author by, 117–18
  in marriage bed, 27–28
  ridding self of fear, 117, 118
Pomcranre, William, 48
Premonition:
  dream, 41–42
  exercise, 37–38
    correlations, 38
    hunches, prediction with, 37–38
    intellect, predictions with, 37
    meditation form 37–38
  points to remember:
    as guide, 173
    importance of, 173
    laziness, 173
    things to avoid, 173
Pregnancy:
  effects on dreams, 47–49
  fears about child, 47–48
  and precognition, 48–49
Presence in farmhouse, case, 119–25
Projective empathy, 62–63
Psi abilities, 3
Psychology Today, 15
Psychometry, 38–40
  attitudes for, 39
  feelings, reactions to, 39–40
  nature, 38
  objects, holding of, 39
  self as instrument, 39
Pyrophoria, 139–40

Reflections from an Angel's Eye, 136
Reincarnation, case:
  Albigensians, 174–77
  remeeting of Steigers, 175
  and Roman Catholic Church, 174–77
Rejuvenation, request for, 170
Revenge of husband's ghost, 141–43
Rhine, J. B., 73

Saltmarsh, H. F., 42
Santayana, George, 194
Schneider, Diana R., 48
Seed, The, 175
Sex:
  frustration of and PK, 130
  involvement, reactions to by seer, 24–25
  loss of interest in, 26
  as power source, 26–27
  repression of, 23–24
Sexual molesters from shadowland:
  cold of sexual organs, 151
  convents hysteria epidemic in, 151
  ethereal semen, 150
  haunted house in Pretoria, South Africa, 149–50
  hermits, 151
  incubi, 150–51
  Lilith, 150
  manifestations, types, 151
  modern incubus, 151–52
  physical semen, 150
  and poltergeists, 153
  protection against, 155–57
  rape/murder haunting, 154
  succubi, 150–51
  zombie ghost, case, 148–49
Sexual satisfaction and Love Force, 200–03
  chakras, 201
  heart chakra, 201–02
  presex, 203
  ritual, 202–03
  sex and love, 202
Shields, Eve, 8–10
Sitwell, Sacheverell, 130
Smith, Alson J., 95
Specious present, concept, 42
Spirit circles, 104–06
  alcohol, 105
  attitudes, 104

darkness, 106
environment, 105
leader, 106
light for, 106
mind state, 106
number of people, 104
number per week, 105
persistence, 105
personnel, 105–06
room for, 104
secretary, 106
setting, 106
smokes, 105
strain, 105
time of day, 105
weather, 105
white light, avoidance of, 106
Spirits, reunion of in spirit world, 96–97
case, 96–97
and marriage, 96
Spying, paranormal, 28
Star People, The, 192
nature of, 192
supposed sound heard by, 192
Starborn Suite, 58
Stearn, Michael, 58
Steiger, Brad, 20ff.
Steiger, Frances P., 4, 37ff.
effects of on husband, 20
Stentor, Norma, 93
Sterling, Allen, 10
Sword of Divine Fire, exercise, 34–35

Tarashanti, 86
Tart, Dr. Charles, 74
Teenagers, and PK, 130
Telepathy:
bereavement, 69
endpoint of healing, 69
healing, 69
nature, 68
ritual for, 68–69
sign of success, 68
techniques, 70–72
use of, 67–69
Telephone lines, PK in, 21
Trance:
assumption of, 108
invitation to the, 108
Transformation:
daily ritual of, 171
violet light of, 171
2001: A Space Odyssey, 192

UFOs:
men-in-black phenomenon, 115–17
appearance of, 115
attitudes to, 116
electrical sabotage, 115–16
eye irritation, 116
and poltergeists, 115–17
reality restructuring, 116–17
threats from, 115
visits from 115
researchers, 114–115
Ullman, Montague, 43

Van de Castle, Dr. R. L., 48

Waddell, Silvia, 89
Waddell, Stanley, 89
Wall, Frances, 63
Wall, Thomas, 63
Wives:
appearance of ghosts of, 138–44
spirit guidance from husband, 144–47
Woodward, Sarah, 29–34

210